Guiding T[

In Washington

2nd Edition

LEGAL AND PRACTICAL THINGS
YOU NEED TO DO TO
SETTLE AN ESTATE IN WASHINGTON

and

HOW TO ARRANGE YOUR OWN AFFAIRS
TO PRESERVE YOUR ASSETS
AND PROVIDE FOR YOUR FAMILY

By AMELIA E. POHL, ESQ.
and
Washington attorney
BENJAMIN G. PORTER

 EAGLE PUBLISHING COMPANY OF BOCA

The purpose of this book is to provide the reader with an informative overview of the subject; but laws change frequently and are subject to different interpretations as courts rule on the meaning or effect of a law. This book is sold with the understanding that neither the authors, nor the editors, nor the publisher, nor the distributors of this book are engaging in, or rendering, legal, accounting, financial planning, medical, or any other professional service. If you need legal, accounting, medical, financial planning or any other expert advice, then you should seek the services of a licensed professional.

This book is intended for use by the consumer for his or her own benefit. If you use this book to counsel someone about the law or tax matters, then that may be considered to be an unauthorized and illegal practice.

WEB SITES: Web sites appear throughout the book. These Web sites are offered for the convenience of the reader only. Publication of these Web site addresses is not an endorsement by the authors, editors or publishers of this book.

EAGLE PUBLISHING COMPANY OF BOCA
4199 N. Dixie Highway, #2
Boca Raton, FL   33431   E-mail: info@eaglepublishing.com

Printed in the United States of America
ISBN 1-892407-71-X
Library of Congress Catalog Card Number: 2001088893

Amelia E. Pohl, Esq.

Before becoming an attorney in 1985, AMELIA E. POHL taught mathematics on both the high school and college level. During her tenure as Associate Professor of Mathematics at Prince George's Community College in Maryland, she wrote several books including

Probability: A Set Theory Approach
Principals of Counting
Common Stock Sense.

During her practice of law Attorney Pohl observed that many people want to reduce the high cost of legal fees by performing or assisting with their own legal transactions. Attorney Pohl found that, with a bit of guidance, people are able to perform many legal transactions for themselves. Attorney Pohl utilizes her background as teacher, author and attorney to provide that "bit of guidance" to the general public in the form of self-help legal books that she has written. Amelia E. Pohl is currently "translating" this book for the remaining 49 states:

Guiding Those Left Behind in Maine
Guiding Those Left Behind In North Dakota
Guiding Those Left Behind In Wyoming, etc.

Benjamin G. Porter, Esq.

BENJAMIN G. PORTER holds a Bachelor of Business Administration (B.B.A) degree from the University of Wisconsin, and a Masters in Laws (Taxation) LL.M degree from Georgetown University Law Center.

Mr. Porter is admitted to practice in the U.S. Federal Court, the U.S. Supreme Court and the U.S. Tax Court. He is a member of the Wisconsin State Board of Governors. He served in the U.S. Army Reserve as Colonel in the Judge Advocate General's Corps.

Mr. Porter is a member of the King County Bar Association., the Washington State Bar Association, the Wisconsin State Bar Association, the Illinois State Bar Association and the American Bar Association. He is a member of several civic organizations, and is past president of the Seattle Sunrise Rotary.

Mr. Porter is a partner with the law firm of PORTER, KOHLI & LeMASTER, P.S. The firm has attorneys who are experienced in estate planning, civil litigation, employment, and business transactions.

Mr. Porter represents individuals and companies in the fields of real estate, business matters, Elder Law, estate and tax planning, including the formation of family Limited Liability Companies (L.L.C.'s) and family and other trusts.

For more information about Mr. Porter and the firm visit their Web site: www.porterkohli.com

THE DESIGN ARTIST

LUBOSH CECH designed the cover of this book. He is a renowned artist, with extensive educational background and professional work experience. He studied design, applied art, and painting in his native Prague, Czech Republic. Just before graduating from the Ph.D. program in art history at the Charles University in Prague, he defected to Italy to escape the political persecution of the communist government. While in Italy, he studied at the University of Bologna.

Since moving to the United States in 1984, Mr. Cech has been designing art exhibitions, working as an art director, and graphic designer. Mr. Cech is a photographer and often incorporates his photographs into his art work.

Lubosh Cech is the founder of OKO DESIGN STUDIO located in Portland, Oregon. He designs promotional materials for print and digital media. He has received numerous rewards for both graphic design and painting. For more information about Mr. Cech and the OKO Design Studio visit his Web site.

http://www.okodesignstudio.com

THE PHOTOGRAPHER

The photograph that appears on the cover was taken by photographer GENE OSON.

The Organization of the Book

If you are going to GUIDE THOSE LEFT BEHIND, you need to know what is involved in settling an estate in Washington, so we begin the book explaining that process. The first six chapters explain:

1. How to tend to the funeral and burial
2. What agencies need to be notified of the death
3. How to locate the decedent's property
4. What bills need (and do not need) to be paid
5. Determining who are the beneficiaries
6. Getting the decedent's property to the proper beneficiary

We devoted a chapter to each of these 6 steps, and for those who are in the process of settling an estate, we placed a CHECK LIST at the end of Chapter 6 to assist in remembering things that need to be done.

Once you read Chapters 1 through 6 you will be able to identify those problems that can occur when someone dies. Using those Chapters as a base, the rest of the book explains how to set up your own Estate Plan so that your family is not burdened by similar problems.

GLOSSARY

This book is designed for the average reader. Legal terminology has been kept to a minimum. There is a glossary at the end of the book in the event you come across a legal term that is not familiar to you.

FICTITIOUS NAMES AND EVENTS

The examples in this book are based loosely on actual events; however, all names are fictitious and the events, as portrayed, are fictitious.

Guiding Those Left Behind
In Washington

CONTENTS

About The Book

We tried to make this book as comprehensive as possible so there are specialized sections of the book that do not apply to the general population and may not be of interest to you. The following GUIDE POSTS appear throughout the book. You can read the section if the situation applies to you or skip the section if it doesn't. Skipping a section will not affect the continuity of the book.

GUIDE POSTS

 The SPOUSE POST means that the information provided is specifically for the spouse of the decedent. If the decedent was single, then skip this section.

 The CALL-A-LAWYER POST alerts you to a situation that may require the assistance of an attorney. See page x for information about how to find a lawyer.

 The CAUTION POST alerts you to a potential problem. It is followed by a suggestion about how to avoid the problem.

 The SPECIAL SITUATION POST means that the information given in that paragraph applies to a particular event or situation; for example when the decedent dies a violent death. If the situation does not apply in your case, you can skip the section.

Reading the Law

Where applicable, we identified the state statute or federal statute that is the basis of the discussion. We did this as a reference, and also to encourage the general public to read the law as it is written. Prior to the Internet the only way you could look up the law was to physically take yourself to the local courthouse law library or the law section of a public library. Today all of the state and federal statutes are literally at your finger tips. They are just a mouse click away on the Internet. To look up a statute all you need is the address of the Web site and the identifying number of the statute:

 WASHINGTON STATUTE WEB SITE
http://www.leg.wa.gov/wsladm

FEDERAL STATUTE WEB SITE
http://www4.law.cornell.edu/uscode

Washington has revised its system of laws (its "Code") into 91 Titles, starting with Title 1: General Provisions and ending with Title 91: Waterways. Much of our discussion deals with Title 11: Probate and Trust Law.

Each Title of the Washington Revised Code is divided into chapters and each chapter into sections. For example (RCW 11.62.010) refers to Title 11, Chapter 62, Section 010 of the Revised Code of Washington.

If you come across a topic that is of importance to you, then you may find it both interesting and profitable to read the law as it is actually written.

When You Need A Lawyer

The purpose of the book is to give the reader an overview of what needs to be done when someone dies, and to provide information about how a person can arrange his own affairs to avoid problems for his own family. It is not intended as a substitute for legal counsel or any other kind of professional advice. If you have any legal question, then you should to seek the counsel of an attorney. When looking for an attorney, consider three things:
EXPERTISE, COST and PERSONALITY.

EXPERTISE

The state of Washington does not have a program to certify that an attorney is specialized in a particular area of law. This being the case an attorney in Washington may not represent to the public that he/she is a "specialist" in any given area of law. Attorneys are allowed to state that they concentrate on certain areas of law. The Washington State Bar Association does not have a lawyer referral service but they can refer you to a county Bar Association who can refer you to someone in your area who practices in the field of law that you seek. Their telephone number is (206) 727-8200, or you can visit their Web site for telephone numbers of local Bar Associations.

 WASHINGTON STATE BAR ASSOCIATION
http://www.wsba.org/

One of the most reliable ways of finding an attorney is through personal referral. Ask your friends, family or business acquaintances if they used an attorney for the field of law that you seek and whether they were pleased with the results. It is important to employ an attorney who is experienced in the area of law you seek. Your friend may have a wonderful Estate Planning attorney, but if you suffered an injury to your body, you need an attorney who is experienced in Personal Injury.

Before employing an attorney for a job, ask how long he has practiced that type of law and what percentage of his practice is devoted to that type of law. Ask whether the attorney has any special training or special degrees in the field of law that you seek.

COST

In addition to the attorney's experience, it is important to check out what to expect to pay in attorney's fees. When you call for an appointment ask what the attorney will charge for the initial consultation and the approximate cost for the service you seek. Ask whether there will be any additional costs such as filing fees, accounting fees, expert witness fees, etc.

If the least expensive attorney is out of your price range then there are many state and private agencies throughout the state that provide legal assistance for people of low income. You can look up the nearest Legal Service or Pro Bono Program in your telephone book, or you can call the Washington State Bar Pro Bono Program at (206) 727-8282 for the telephone number of legal service program in your county.

The American Bar Association has a list of Washington Legal Services Programs at the General Public Resources section of its Web site:

   AMERICAN BAR ASSOCIATION WEB SITE
   http://www.abanet.org

PERSONALITY

Of equal importance to the attorney's experience and legal fees, is your relationship with the attorney. How easy was it to reach the attorney? Did you go through lay-ers of   receptionists and legal assistants before being allowed to speak to the attorney? Did the attorney promptly return your call? If you had difficulty reaching the attorney,   then you can expect similar problems should you employ that attorney.

Did the attorney treat you with respect? Did the attorney treat you paternally with a "father knows best" attitude or did the attorney treat you as an intelligent person with the ability to understand the options available to you and the ability to make your own decision based on the information provided to you. Are you able to understand and easily communicate with the attorney? Is he speaking in plain English or is his explanation of the matter so full of legalese to be almost meaningless to you?

Do you find the attorney's personality to be pleasant or grating? Sometimes people rub each other the wrong way. It is like rubbing a cat the wrong way. Stroking a cat from head to tail is pleasing to the cat, but petting it in the opposite direction, no matter how well intended, causes friction. If the lawyer makes you feel annoyed or uncomfortable, then find another attorney.

It is worth the effort to take the time to interview as many attorneys as it takes to find one with the right expertise, fee schedule and personality for you.

The First Week

Dealing with the death of a close family member or friend is difficult. Not only do you need to deal with your own emotions, but often with those of your family and friends. Sometimes their sorrow is more painful to you, than what you are experiencing yourself.

In addition to the emotional impact of a death, there are many things that need to be done, from arranging the funeral and burial, to closing out the business affairs of the *decedent* (the person who died) and finally giving whatever property is left to the proper beneficiary.

The funeral and burial take only a few days. Wrapping up the affairs of the decedent may take considerably longer. This chapter explains what things you (the spouse or closest family member) need to do during the first week, beginning at the moment of death and continuing through the funeral.

 MALE GENDER USED

Rather than use "he/she" or "his/her" for simplicity
(and hoping not to offend anyone)
we will refer to the decedent, the
Personal Representative, and his attorney
using the male gender.

References to other people will be in both genders.

AUTOPSIES

In today's high tech world of medicine, doctors are fairly certain of the cause of death, but if there is a question, the doctor may ask permission to perform an autopsy. There is an order of priority to authorize the procedure:

1st	The spouse	2nd	An adult child
3rd	Either parent	4th	An adult brother or sister
5th	A court appointed guardian		
6th	Anyone authorized to dispose of the body		

Reasonable efforts must be made to find the person with highest authority because the autopsy cannot be performed if permission is granted and someone with higher authority objects (RCW 68.50.101). The person giving authorization must agree to pay for the autopsy because the cost is not covered under most health insurance plans.

The cost of an autopsy can run anywhere from several hundred to several thousand dollars, but it is in the family's best interest to consent to the autopsy. The examination might reveal a genetic disorder that could be treated if it later appears in another family member. Death from a car "accident" could have been a heart attack at the wheel. Perhaps the patient who died suddenly in a hospital was misdiagnosed. The nursing home resident could have died from negligence and not old age.

Even if none of these are found, knowing the cause of death with certainty is better than not knowing.

That was the case with the family of a woman who was taken to the hospital complaining of stomach pains. The doctors thought she might be suffering from gallbladder disease but she died before they could effectively treat her. A doctor suggested that an autopsy be performed to determine the actual cause of death.

The woman had three daughters, one of whom objected to the autopsy "Why spend that kind of money? It won't bring Mom back."

The daughter's wishes were respected; however, over the years as they aged and became ill with their own various ailments, they would undergo physical examinations. As part of taking their medical history, doctors routinely asked "And what was the cause of your mother's death?"

None could answer the question.

This is not a dramatic story. No mysterious genetic disorder ever occurred in any of the daughters, nor in any of their children. But each daughter (including the one who objected) at some point in her life, was confronted with the nagging question "What did Mom die of?"

MANDATORY AUTOPSIES

When a person dies, a physician must sign the death certificate stating the cause of death. If a person dies in a hospital, then there is a doctor present to sign the certificate. If a person who is terminally ill, dies at home while under the care of a physician or a hospice worker, then in most cases, no emergency vehicle need be called. The treating physician needs to be notified of the death, and he will sign the death certificate.

If a person who was not under the care of a physician, dies suddenly at home, or if someone dies through accident, foul play or suicide, then the police must be notified. The person who discovers the body should call 911 to summon the police. The police will have the Coroner take charge of the body.

The Coroner or Medical Examiner will perform an autopsy whenever there is a suspicion that the death was not from natural causes or that the death was caused by a disease that might pose a threat to public health. The cost of performing the autopsy is paid by the county conducting the procedure (RCW 36.24.190, 68.50.010, 68.50.104).

AUTOPSIES PERFORMED BY THE INSURANCE COMPANY

An insurance company that issues an accident or sickness policy in the state of Washington has the right to conduct an autopsy. The cost of the autopsy is paid by the insurance company, so they will not do so unless there is good reason for the examination (RCW 48.20.132 48.21.100).

ANATOMICAL GIFTS

If, before death, the decedent made an anatomical gift by signing a donor card or by giving his Agent authority to make the gift as part of a Power of Attorney, then hospital personnel or the donor's doctor need to be made aware of the gift in quick proximity to the time of death — preferably before death.

GIFT AUTHORIZED BY THE FAMILY

Hospital personnel determine whether a mortally ill patient is a candidate for an organ donation. Early on in the donor program those over 65 were not considered as suitable candidates. Today, however, the condition of the organ, and not the age, is the determining factor.

The federal government has established regional Organ Procurement Organizations throughout the United States, to coordinate the donor program. The Organ Procurement Organization in state of Washington is located in Bellevue, Washington. It is called LifeCenter Northwest. If it is determined that a patient is a candidate, the hospital will contact Lifecenter Northwest.

LifeCenter Northwest will determine whether the patient is a suitable donor. If they decide to request the gift, and the candidate did not sign a donor card, then someone in the family must give written permission. Someone who is specially trained will approach the family to request the donation (RCW 68.50.500).

Washington statute RCW 68.50.550 establishes an order of priority to authorize the donation:

1st The court appointed guardian of the person of the decedent at time of death (if any)

2nd A person appointed by the decedent in a durable power of attorney to make his health care decisions

3rd The spouse

4th A son or daughter who is at least 18

5th Either parent

6th A brother or sister who is at least 18

7th A grandparent of the decedent

If permission is obtained from a family member and there are others in the same or a higher priority, then an effort must be made to contact those people and get their approval. For example, if the brother of the decedent agrees to the gift (6th in priority) and the decedent had an adult son (4th in priority), then the son needs to be made aware of the gift. If the son objects, no gift can be made. Similarly, the statute prohibits the gift if the decedent ever expressed his opposition to a donation.

AFTER THE DONATION

Once the donation is made the body is delivered to the funeral home and prepared for burial or cremation as directed by the family. The donation does not disfigure the body so there can be an open casket viewing if the family so wishes.

For privacy reasons, the identity of the donor and the recipient of the gift is not disclosed, but on request from the donor's or recipient's family, most Organ Procurement Organizations will give basic demographic information such as the age, sex, marital status, number of children and occupation of the donor or recipient of the gift.

Guiding Those Left Behind In Washington

GIFT FOR EDUCATION OR RESEARCH

If the decedent signed a donor card indicating his wish to use his body for any purpose and he is not a candidate for an organ donation, then you can offer to release the body for education or research. If you live in the western half of the state, then contact:

University of Washington   (206) 543-1860
Department of Biological Structure
Seattle, WA   98195-7420

If you live in the eastern half of the state, contact:

Washington State University   (509) 335-2602
School of Medicine, Department of Anatomy
Pullman, WA   99164-3510

You will need to call the school to determine whether they will accept the body. Most schools will not accept bodies from those who have died from a contagious disease or from crushing injuries or who are extremely obese.

There is no fee to the family to make the donation. The school will pay for the cost of transportation of the body to the institution, provided the body is in the local area of the university

The study usually takes 18 months to two years. Once it is complete, the body is cremated and the *cremains* (cremated remains) are returned to the family, or if the family wishes, the cremains can be buried at the university burial site.

MAKING THE DONATION

An anatomical gift may be made to any hospital, physician, accredited medical or dental school, as well as any bank or storage facility. It is not legal for anyone to purchase body parts. It is legal to charge the recipient monies to prepare, store, and transport bodies or body parts (RCW 68.50.610).

Non-for-profit and as well as for-profit companies have sprung up that are in the business of preparing and delivering body parts. These companies ask families for donations (so they are not buying body parts). The company prepares the body tissue or other parts of the body, and then distributes the parts throughout the United States to physicians, hospitals, research centers, etc. In many cases the monies charged for preparation and transportation includes a sizable profit. If someone other than LifeCenter Northwest (the Washington Organ Procurement Organization) approaches you to make a donation, then before agreeing to the donation you may want to learn about the company making the request:
> What is the name of the company?
> Where are their main headquarters located?
> What is their primary business activity?
> What is the name and job description of the
> person making the request?

DETERMINE THE END USE OF THE DONATION

You may want to ask what they intend to do with the tissue or body part. If it is being used for research, then what type of research? Where is the research being conducted? If it will be used for transplantation, then what agency (doctor, hospital) will receive the donation and where is that agency located? Once you have this in-formation you can make an informed decision as to whether you wish to make the donation to that organization.

THE FUNERAL

Approximately ten percent of deaths occur suddenly because of accident, suicide, foul play or undetected illness. But, in general, death occurs after a lengthy illness, with a common scenario being that of an aged person who dies after being ill for several months, if not years. In such case, family and friends are emotionally prepared for the happening. Expected or not, the first job is the disposition of the body.

THE PREARRANGED FUNERAL

Increasingly, people are arranging, in advance, for their own funeral and burial. This makes it easier on the family both financially and emotionally. All the decisions have been made and there is no guessing what the decedent would have wanted.

If the decedent made provision for his burial, then you should come across a burial certificate, or perhaps a deed to a burial space. If he arranged for his funeral, then you should find a funeral contract. You need to read the contract to determine what provisions were made. If the contract was paid on an installment basis, you need to determine whether it is paid in full. You also need to determine whether the contract was a fixed price agreement or whether there will be additional charges.

If you cannot locate the contract, but you know the decedent made provision for his funeral, then call the funeral home and ask them to send you a copy of the contract. If you believe the decedent purchased a funeral plan but you do not know the name of the funeral home, then call the local funeral homes. Many local funeral homes are owned by national firms with computer capacity to identify people who have purchased a contract at any of their many locations.

Once you have possession of the contract, take it with you to the funeral home and go over the terms of the contract with the funeral director. Inquire whether there is any charge that is not included in the contract.

MAKING FUNERAL ARRANGEMENTS

If the decedent died unexpectedly or without having made any prior funeral arrangements then your first job is to choose a funeral director and make arrangements for the funeral or cremation. Most people choose the nearest or most conveniently located funeral home without comparison shopping. However prices for these services can vary significantly from funeral home to funeral home. Savings can be had if you take the time to make a few phone calls.

Receiving price quotes by telephone is your right under both state and federal law. Federal Trade Commission ("FTC") Rule 453.2 (b) (1) and requires a funeral director to give an accurate telephone quote of the prices of his goods and services. This rule is also required under state law (RCW 18.39.195). Funeral firms are listed in the telephone directory under FUNERAL DIRECTORS. If you live in a small town, there may be only one or two listings, so you may need to make calls to the next largest city.

Funeral directors usually provide the following services:
➤ arrange for the transportation of the body
  to the funeral home and then to the burial site
➤ obtain burial transit permits
➤ arrange for the embalming or cremation of the body
➤ arrange funeral and memorial services
➤ obtain information for the death certificate
➤ order copies of the death certificate for the family.

To compare prices you will need to determine:

✧ what is included in the price of a basic funeral plan

✧ whether you can expect any additional cost.

If the decedent did not own a burial space, then that cost must be included when making funeral arrangements.

It may be necessary to have the body embalmed if you are going to have a viewing. Embalming is not necessary if you order a direct cremation or an immediate burial without a viewing. Federal Trade Commission Rule 453.5 prohibits the funeral home from charging an embalming fee unless you order the service.

PURCHASING THE CASKET

When comparison-shopping, you will find that the single most expensive item to be a casket. When selecting a casket you need to be aware that there may be a considerable mark-up in the price quoted by the funeral director. You do not need to go "sole source" when purchasing the casket. If you feel that the price quoted by the funeral director is too high, you can purchase the casket elsewhere and have it delivered to the funeral home to be used instead of the one offered by the funeral director. Federal regulations require a funeral home to accept a casket that is purchased elsewhere.

The funeral director must provide you with a written price list at the beginning of your discussion of funeral arrangements. If the price list given to you by the funeral home states that the price of their casket includes a specific dollar amount for basic services, and you do not purchase the casket from the funeral home, then the funeral director is allowed to add that specific dollar amount to the charge for his basic services. He is not allowed to charge a handling fee for accepting a casket that is purchased elsewhere (FTC Rule 453.2, 453.4).

Of course the problem with purchasing a casket is that most of us have no idea what to pay. Caskets are not usually displayed for sale in a shopping mall, so how do you determine the going price? The answer is the Internet. You can learn all about the cost of any item, even a casket, by using your search engine to find a retail casket sales dealer. If you are not computer literate, you can locate the nearest retail casket sales outlet by looking in the yellow pages under CASKETS. You may need to look in the telephone directory for the nearest large city to find a listing. By making a call to a retail casket sales dealer, you will become knowledgeable in the price range of caskets. You can then decide what is a reasonable price for the product you seek.

The best time to do your comparison shopping, is before you go to the funeral home to arrange for the funeral. Once you have determined what you should pay for the casket, it is only fair to give the funeral director the opportunity to meet that price. If you cannot reach a meeting of the minds, then you can always order the casket from the retail sales dealer and have it delivered to the funeral home.

ON-LINE FUNERAL SERVICES

The Internet is changing the way the world does business, and the funeral industry is no exception. A growing number of mortuaries are offering live Webcasts of funerals and wakes for those who are unable to pay their respects in person.

There are Web sites such as ObitDetails.com where you can post an obituary. There are on-line memorial chat rooms as well as online eulogies and testimonials. There is even a Web site that offers a posthumous e-mail service which allows people to leave final messages for friends and relatives.

THE CREMATION

Increasingly people are opting for cremation. Based on statistics published by the Washington state Department of Health, over 60% of those who die in Washington are cremated each year. And that percentage is growing. The reasons for choosing cremation are varied, but for the majority, it is a matter of finances. The cost of cremation is approximately one-sixth that of an ordinary funeral and burial. A major saving is the cost of the casket. No casket is necessary for the cremation and Federal law prohibits a Funeral Director from saying that a casket is required for a direct cremation (FTC Rule 453.3 (b)ii). You may need a suitable container to deliver the body to the crematory. After the cremation, you will need an urn for the ashes.

If you are having a memorial service in a place of worship and no viewing of the body before the cremation, then consider contracting with a facility that does cremations only. Look in the telephone book under CREMATION SERVICES. You will also see cremation "societies" in the telephone book. Some are for-profit and others non-profit. You can also find advertisements for cremation services on the Internet. These cremation facilities provide much the same services as a funeral home but with one important exception — the cremation service does not provide any type of funeral service or public viewing of the body.

THE OVERWEIGHT DECEDENT

If the decedent weighs more than 300 pounds, then you need to check to see if the cremation service has facilities large enough to handle the body. You will need to make burial arrangements if you cannot locate a crematory that can accommodate the body.

DECEDENT WITH PACEMAKER

Cremating a body with a pacemaker or any radiation producing devise can cause damage to the cremation chamber or to the person performing the cremation. If the decedent was wearing such electronic aid, then you need to investigate the cost of having it removed prior to the cremation. The cremation service director may be able help you to arrange for the removal of the device. A used pacemaker can be donated to an animal treatment center for treatment for a dog with heart disease. If you wish to make a donation you can contact a local veterinarian, who may offer to remove the device without charge to you.

DISPOSING OF THE ASHES

Once cremated, the decedent's remains can be placed in a cemetery. Many cemeteries have a separate building called a *columbarium*, which is especially designed to store urns. The cremains can also be placed in a cemetery plot. Some cemeteries allow the cremains of a family member to be placed in an occupied family plot. Similarly, some cemeteries will allow urns to be placed in a space in a mausoleum currently occupied by a member of the decedent's family. If you wish to have the cremains placed in an occupied mausoleum or family plot, then you need to call the cemetery and ask them to explain their policy as it relates to the burial of urns in occupied sites.

SCATTERED AT SEA

The decedent may have expressed a desire to have his ashes placed at sea. The funeral director or cremation direction should be able to assist you in seeing to it that these wishes are respected. Federal law prohibits the ashes from being scattered any closer than 3 nautical miles from land, so you will need to arrange to have a boat carry the ashes out to sea (Code of Federal Regulations, Title 40, Section 229.1).

It sometimes happens that the decedent is cremated and no one comes back to pick the cremains. In such case the crematory will hold the cremains for 2 years and dispose of them in any legal manner. Similarly, someone may have a body delivered to a funeral home and then never come back to arrange for its final disposition. After a year, the funeral home has the right to dispose of the body and bill the next of kin for the service.

Washington law holds the following people responsible for the disposition of the body.

1. the surviving spouse
2. the decedent's adult children
3. the surviving parents
4. the surviving siblings
5. anyone appointed by the decedent to act as his representative.

Responsibility to dispose of the body, and pay for such disposition, is in the order given. If there is more than one person in a given class, then each, individually, is responsible for payment and all of them together are responsible to pay for the disposition (RCW 68.50.160, 68.50.230).

THE OUT OF STATE BURIAL

If the decedent is to be buried in another state, the body will need to be transported to that state. Most funeral homes belong to a national network of funeral homes and can help you with arrangements in that state. If services are to be held in Washington and in another state, then your local funeral director can make arrangements with the out-of-state funeral home for the transportation of the body. If you do not wish to employ a local funeral director, you can contact the out-of-state funeral director and have him/her make arrangement with the airline for the transportation of the body.

If the body has been cremated, then you can transport the cremains yourself, either by carrying the ashes as part of your luggage or by arranging with the airline to transport the ashes as cargo. Have a certified copy of the death certificate available in the event that you need to identify the remains of the decedent.

In these days of heightened security, it is important to call the airline before departure and ask whether they have any special regulation or procedure regarding the transportation of human ashes.

SPOUSE　　THE MILITARY BURIAL

Subject to availability of burial spaces, an honorably discharged veteran and/or his unmarried minor or handicapped child and/or his un-remarried spouse may be buried in a national military cemetery. Some cemeteries have room only for cremated remains or for the casketed remains of a family member of someone who is currently buried in that cemetery, so you need to call for space availability.

There is one national military cemetery located in Washington:

Tahoma National Cemetery
18600 Southeast 240th Street
Kent, WA   98042-4868
Telephone: (425) 413-9614

The Department of the Army is in charge of the Arlington National Cemetery. If you wish to have an eligible deceased veteran buried in the Arlington National Cemetery, then call them at (703) 695-3250.

Arlington National Cemetery
Interment Service Branch
Arlington, VA   22211

THE COST OF A MILITARY BURIAL

Burial space in a National Cemetery is free of charge. Cemetery employees will open and close the grave and mark it with a headstone or grave marker without cost to the family. If requested, the local Veteran's Administration ("VA") will provide the family with a memorial flag. The VA will not pay to have the body transported to the cemetery, so the family needs to make funeral arrangements with a funeral firm and have them transport the remains to the cemetery.

Regardless of where an honorably discharged veteran is buried, allowances may be available for the plot, and the burial and grave marker expenses. The amount varies depending on factors such as whether the veteran died because of a service related injury. The VA will not reimburse any burial or funeral expense for the spouse of a veteran.

For information about reimbursement of funeral and burial expenses you can call the VA at (800) 827-1000.

The Department of Veteran's Affairs has a Web site with information on the following topics:

- ➢ National and Military Cemeteries
- ➢ Burial, Headstones and Markers
- ➢ State Cemetery Grants Program
- ➢ Obtaining Military Records
- ➢ Locating Veterans

 VA CEMETERY WEB SITE
http://www.cem.va.gov

BENEFITS FOR SPOUSE OF DECEDENT VETERAN

SPOUSE

The surviving spouse of an honorably discharged veteran should contact the Veteran's Administration to determine whether he/she is eligible for any benefits. For example, if the decedent had minor or disabled children, his spouse may also be eligible for a monthly benefit of Dependency and Indemnity Compensation ("DIC"). If the Veteran's surviving spouse receives nursing home care under Medicaid, then the spouse might be eligible for monthly payments from the VA.

Whether a surviving spouse is eligible for any of these benefits depends on many factors including whether the decedent was serving on active duty, whether his death was service related, and the surviving spouse's assets and income. DIC benefits are discontinued should the surviving spouse remarry; however, the law permits payments to be resumed in the event that the subsequent marriage ends because of death or divorce.

For information about whether the surviving spouse is eligible for any benefit related to the decedent's military service call the VA at (800) 827-1000. You can receive a printed statement of public policy: VA Pamphlet 051-000-00217-2 FEDERAL BENEFITS FOR VETERANS AND DEPENDENTS by sending a check in the amount of $5 to
THE SUPERINTENDENT OF DOCUMENTS
P.O. Box 371954
Pittsburgh, PA 15250-7954
Information is also available at the VA Web site:

VA WEB SITE
http://www.va.gov

Police will try to locate the family of an indigent resident who dies in their city or county. If the family of the decedent cannot be found or if the family is unable to arrange for his burial, then the county Coroner or Medical Examiner will arrange for the disposition of the body. The Coroner will send the body to a local funeral home. The choice of funeral home is on a rotating basis for those firms who wish to participate in the program (RCW 36.24.155, 36.39.030).

THE INDIGENT VETERAN

As explained on the previous page, the federal government provides a free burial space of the honorably discharged Veteran. The surviving spouse or minor child might be eligible for financial assistance with funeral and burial expenses as well. If the Veteran was indigent, the Commanding Officer of any post, camp or chapter of any national organization of Veterans, (such as the American Legion) can ask the county for financial assistance for the funeral. The county legislative authority sets the maximum amount that can be given. Washington statute requires that at least $300 be given.

This assistance extends to the minor child, spouse or widow(er) of a Veteran, namely if there are no funds to bury the Veteran's minor child or spouse or widow(er), the relief committee of any post, camp or chapter, can ask the county for assistance with funeral expenses (RCW 73.08.070)

THE VIOLENT OR WRONGFUL DEATH

If the decedent died a violent death or under circumstances in which foul play is suspected, the Coroner will take possession of the body. The body will not be released to the funeral director until the examination of the body is complete. In the interim, the family can proceed with arrangements for the funeral. The funeral director will contact the Coroner to determine when he can pick up the body and proceed with the funeral.

THE WRONGFUL DEATH
If the decedent's death was caused by a wrongful act, the person settling the Estate; i.e., the *Personal Representative*, can sue for a wrongful death, regardless of whether the wrongdoer is convicted of a crime. The law suit must be filed within 3 years of the decedent's death. Monies awarded by the jury will go to the surviving spouse, child or stepchild. If there is no spouse or child, the Personal Representative can sue for the benefit of the decedent's parents or sisters or brothers who were dependent on the decedent for support and who lived in the United States at the time of the death (RCW 4.16.080, 4.20.010, 4.20.020).

WORK RELATED DEATH
Consult your attorney about applying for death benefits relating to the decedent's job. The state of Washington provides significant benefits to the spouse and/or dependent members of the families of government employees, such as policemen and firemen, who die during the performance of their duties. Other workers may be covered by Worker's Compensation (RCW 41.24.160, 41.44.210, 51.32.050).

Special Situation ⟩ CRIME VICTIMS COMPENSATION

The Washington CRIME VICTIMS COMPENSATION PROGRAM assists family and dependents of a person who died as a result of a crime. Compensation is available for lost wages, funeral, medical and dental expenses, psychological counseling, etc. A surviving spouse or child may be eligible for limited pension payments. The amount of compensation varies depending on the circumstance. The most that can be paid for a death is $40,000. To be eligible for compensation a family member must apply within 2 years and the following must be true:

➤ The decedent was an innocent victim;

➤ The applicant cooperated with law enforcement officers to apprehend or convict the perpetrator;

➤ The decedent was not in a correctional facility at the time of the crime or in any facility maintained by the Department of Social and Health Services.

The applicant needs to seek compensation from all other sources such as health or life insurance, or workers' compensation. Any amount received from these sources may reduce the amount awarded (RCW 7.68.060, 7.68.070, 7.68.130). You can get an application from your local Victim/Witness Office or by calling (800) 762-3716 or by writing to:

CRIME VICTIMS COMPENSATION PROGRAM
P.O. Box 44520
Olympia, WA 98504-4520

Information and telephone numbers of local Victim/Witness Offices can be found on the Internet.

 CRIME VICTIMS COMPENSATION
http://www.ocva.wa.gov/cvcp.html

 **LAWYER** THE MISSING BODY

Few things are more difficult to deal with than a missing person. The emotional turmoil created by the "not knowing" is often more difficult than the finality of death. The legal problems created by the disappearance are also more difficult than if the person simply died. It may take a two-part legal process — the appointment of a Trustee to manage the missing person's property, and then another Court procedure to distribute his property once the Court rules that the person is, or is presumed, to be dead (RCW 11.80.010).

APPOINTING A TRUSTEE

An *Absentee* is a person who is missing and who cannot be found after a diligent search. If the Absentee has financial matters that need attending (bills that need to be paid, family to support, etc.), then anyone affected by the disappearance can ask the Superior Court to be appointed as Trustee to care for and manage the Absentee's property. An attorney experienced in Probate matters will need to be employed to assist in presenting evidence to the Court that the Absentee is missing, and then having the Trustee appointed.

DISTRIBUTING THE PROPERTY

Anyone who has the right to inherit the Absentee's property can for ask for a distribution of the property anytime there is sufficient evidence that the Absentee is dead or after 7 years have passed. The Court may allow a provisional distribution of the property after 5 years, but will require a bond in the event the Absentee is found before the 7 year wait ends (RCW 11.80.090, 11.80.100).

THE PROBLEM
FUNERAL OR BURIAL

The funeral and burial industry is well regulated by the state and federal government. The following acts are some of the acts subject to disciplinary action:

⊠ Using a used casket for burial without the customer's written consent

⊠ Using a false or misleading advertisement

⊠ Paying kick-backs to generate business

⊠ Having diminished capacity because of alcohol, controlled substances, or even using prescription drugs that impairs performance

⊠ Violating any federal or state law relating to funeral practice

⊠ Providing financial or investment advice when performing funeral or burial services (RCW 18.39.220, 18.39.231 18.39.410).

Funeral directors are licensed professionals so it is unusual to have a problem with the funeral or burial or cremation. If, however, you had a bad experience with any aspect of the funeral then you can file a complaint with the state licensing agency:

Department of Licensing
Funeral and Cemetery Licensing Program
P.O. Box 9012
Olympia, WA 98507-9012
Telephone (360) 586-4905

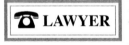

In addition to filing a complaint with the Board, you may wish to consult with an attorney who is experienced in litigation matters to learn of any other legal remedy you may have.

THE DEATH CERTIFICATE

It is the job of the funeral director or cremation service director to provide information about the decedent to the Vital Records Department of the of the Washington State Department of Health. The Vital Records Department will prepare a death certificate based on that information. It is important that the information you give to the funeral or cremation director is correct. You need to check the form completed by the funeral or cremation director to be sure names are correctly spelled and dates correctly written. Once the information is submitted to the Vital Records Department, it will be difficult and time consuming to make a correction.

The funeral or cremation director will order as many certified copies of the death certificate as you request. Most establishments require an original certified copy and not a photocopy so you need to order sufficient certified copies. The following is a list of institutions that may want a certified copy:

* Each insurance company that insured the decedent or his property (health insurance, life insurance, etc.)
* Each financial institution in which the decedent had money invested (brokerage houses, banks)
* The decedent's pension fund
* Each credit card company used by the decedent
* The IRS
* The Social Security Administration
* The State Department of Licensing (motor vehicles)
* If Probate is necessary, the Clerk of the Court.

Some airlines and car rental companies offer a discount for short notice, emergency trips. If you have family flying in for the funeral, you may wish to order a few extra copies of the death certificate so that they can obtain an airline or car rental discount.

If you wish to order certified copies of the death certificate at a later date, you can ask the funeral director to do so, or can get a certified copy by writing to:

Washington Department of Health
Center for Health Statistics
P.O. Box 9709
Olympia, WA 98507-9709
Telephone: (360) 236-4313

You will need to call to determine what information they require. The current fee is $13 for each certified copy of the death certificate. Check or money order is made payable to the Department of Health.

It takes several weeks to get a copy, however, you can speed up the process by paying $24 per copy with a credit card. Express mail delivery is an additional $10.00.

You can download the application for a record search and for a certified copy of the death record from the Internet.

 WASHINGTON STATE DEPARTMENT OF HEALTH
http://www.doh.wa.gov/

About Probate

Once a person dies, all of the property he owns as of the date of his death is referred to as the *decedent's Estate.* If the decedent owned property that was in his name only (not jointly or in trust for someone) then some sort of court procedure may be necessary to determine who is entitled to possession of the property. The name of the court procedure is *Probate*. In Washington, the Probate procedure is conducted in the Superior Court. The root of the word Probate is "to prove." It refers to the first job of the Court, that is, to examine proof of whether the decedent left a valid Will. The second job of the Court is to appoint someone to wrap up the affairs of the decedent — to pay any outstanding bills and then to distribute what property is left to the beneficiaries.

If the decedent left a valid Will naming someone as *Executor* of his Estate, then the Court will appoint that person for the job and issue *Letters Testamentary* giving him authority to administer the Estate. If the decedent died without a Will, then the Court will appoint someone to be the *Administrator* of his Estate and issue *Letters of Administration* (RCW 11.02.005, 11.28.010).

For simplicity, we will refer to the person appointed by the Court to settle the decedent's Estate as the *Personal Representative*, and the document authorizing him to act, as *Letters*. We will refer to the property that is to be distributed as part of a Probate procedure as the decedent's *Probate Estate* and the method of conducting a Probate procedure as the *Estate Administration*.

In Chapter 6 we will explain the different kinds of Estate Administration that are available in the state of Washington. But we are getting ahead of ourselves. First we need to determine whether a Probate procedure is necessary. To answer that question we need to know exactly what the decedent owned, so the next two chapters explain how to identify, and then locate, all of the decedent's assets.

Giving Notice Of The Death 2

Those closest to the decedent usually notify family members and close friends by telephone. The funeral director will arrange to have an obituary published in as many different newspapers as the family requests, but there is still the job of notifying the government and people who were doing business with the decedent. If no Probate procedure is necessary, the job of notifying people of the death falls to his spouse; and in the absence of a spouse, to the decedent's next of kin. By *next of kin,* we mean those people who inherit the decedent's property according to WASHINGTON'S LAWS OF DESCENT AND DISTRIBUTION. Those laws are explained in Chapter 5.

If a probate procedure is necessary then the job of notifying people of the death belongs to the person named as the Personal Representative in the decedent's Will. If the decedent died without a Will, then whoever is appointed as Personal Representative has the job. If no Probate procedure is necessary, then it's up to the next of kin.

The person who has the job of settling the decedent's Estate should begin to give notice as soon as is practicable after the death. Two government agencies that need to be notified are the Social Security Administration and the IRS. This chapter gives their telephone number and other agencies that need to be notified.

NOTIFYING SOCIAL SECURITY

Many Funeral Directors will, as part of their service package, notify the Social Security Administration of the death. You may wish to check to see that this has been done. You can do so by calling (800) 772-1213. If you are hearing impaired call (800) 325-0778 TTY. You will need to give the Social Security Administration the full legal name of the decedent as well as his social security number and date of birth.

Special Situation DECEDENT RECEIVING SOCIAL SECURITY CHECKS

If the decedent was receiving checks from Social Security, then you need to determine whether his last check needs to be returned to the Social Security Administration.

Each Social Security check is a payment for the prior month, provided that person lives for the entire prior month. If someone dies on the last day of the month, then you should not cash the check for that month. For example, if someone dies on July 31st, then you need to return the check that the agency mails out in August. If however, the decedent died on August 1st then the check sent in August need not be returned because that check is payment for the month of July.

If the Social Security check is electronically deposited into a bank account, then notify the bank that the account holder died and notify the Social Security Administration as well. If the check needs to be returned, then the Social Security Administration will withdraw it electronically from the bank account. You will need to keep the account open until the funds are withdrawn.

| SPOUSE |

SPOUSE/CHILD'S
SOCIAL SECURITY BENEFITS

If the decedent had sufficient work credits, the Social Security Administration will give the decedent's widow(er) or if unmarried, then the decedent's minor children, a one-time death benefit in the amount of $255.

SURVIVORS BENEFITS:

The spouse (or ex-spouse) of the decedent may be eligible for Survivors Benefits. Benefits vary depending on the amount of work credits earned by the decedent, whether the decedent had minor or disabled children, the spouse's age, how long they were married, and other factors. The minor child of the decedent may be eligible for benefits regardless of whether the child's father (the decedent) ever married the child's mother. Paternity can be established by any one of several methods including the father acknowledging his child in writing or verbally to members of his family. For more information you can call the Social Security Administration at (800) 772-1213.

SOCIAL SECURITY BENEFITS

A spouse or ex-spouse can collect Social Security benefits based on the decedent's work record. This value may be greater than the spouse now receives. It is important to make an appointment with your local Social Security office and determine whether you as the spouse (or ex-spouse) or parent of the decedent's minor child are eligible for any Social Security or Survivor Benefits. The Social Security Administration has a Web site from which you can download publications that explain Survivors Benefits.

SOCIAL SECURITY ADMINISTRATION
http://www.ssa.gov

DECEDENT WITH
GOVERNMENT PENSION

Any pension or annuity check received after the date of death of a federal retiree, or a survivor annuitant, needs to be returned to the U.S. Treasury. If the check is direct deposited to a bank account, then call the financial institution and ask them to return the check. If the check is sent by mail then you need to return it to:

Director, Regional Finance Center
U. S. Treasury Department
P.O. Box 7367
Chicago, IL 60680

Include a letter explaining the reason for the return of the check and stating the decedent's date of death.

$$$ APPLY FOR BENEFITS $$$

A survivor annuity may be available to a surviving spouse, and/or minor or disabled child. In some cases, a former spouse may be eligible for benefits. Even though you notify the government of the death, they will not automatically give you benefits to which you may be entitled. You need to apply for those benefits by notifying the Office of Personnel Management ("OPM") of the death and requesting that they send you an application for survivor benefits. You can call them at (888) 767-6738 or you can write to:

THE OFFICE OF PERSONNEL MANAGEMENT
SERVICE AND RECORDS CENTER
BOYERS, PA 16017

You will find brochures and information about Survivor's Benefits at the OPM Web site.

U.S. OFFICE OF PERSONNEL MANAGEMENT
http://www.opm.gov

DECEDENT WITH COMPANY PENSION OR ANNUITY

In most cases, pension and annuity checks are payment for the prior month. If the decedent received his pension or annuity check before his death, then no monies need be returned. Pension checks and/or annuity checks received after the date of death may need to be returned to the company. You need to notify the company of the death to determine the status of the last check sent to the decedent.

Before notifying the company, locate the policy or pension statement that is the basis of the income. That document should tell whether there is a beneficiary of the pension or annuity funds now that the pensioner or annuitant is dead. If you cannot locate the document, use the return address on the check envelope and ask the company to send you a copy of the plan. Also request that they forward to you any claim form that may be required in order for the survivor or beneficiary to receive benefits under that pension plan or policy.

If the pension/annuity check is direct deposited to the decedent's account, then ask the bank to assist you in locating the company and notifying the company of the death.

DECEDENT WITH AN IRA or QUALIFIED RETIREMENT PLAN ("QRP")

Anyone who is a beneficiary of an Individual Retirement Account ("IRA") or QRP needs to keep in mind that income taxes may not have been paid on monies placed in an IRA or QRP account. Once monies are withdrawn, significant taxes may be due. You need to learn what options are available to you as a beneficiary of the plan and the tax consequences of each option. You will need to ask an accountant how much will be due in taxes for each option. Once you know all the facts, you will be able to make the best choice for your circumstance.

SPOUSE

There are special options available if the spouse is the beneficary of the decedent's IRA account. The spouse has the right to withdraw the money from the account or roll it over into the spouse's own retirement account. Although the employer can explain options that are available, the spouse still needs to understand the tax consequence of choosing any given option. It is important to consult with an accountant to determine the best way to go.

If the decedent had a QRP, the plan may permit the spouse to roll the balance of the account into a new IRA. The spouse needs to contact the decedent's employer for an explanation of the plan and all the options that are available at this time.

NOTIFYING IRS

The decedent's final federal income tax return (IRS form 1040) needs to be filed by April 15th of the year following the year in which he died. There is no state income tax. If the decedent was married, then the surviving spouse can file a final joint return. If there is no surviving spouse, then it is the Personal Representative's job to file the final return. If no Probate procedure is necessary, then whoever inherits the decedent's property needs to file the final income tax return. If you have a joint bank account with the decedent, you may want to keep the account open until you determine whether the decedent is entitled to an income tax refund. See Chapter 6 for an explanation of how to obtain a refund from the IRS.

THE GOOD NEWS
Monies inherited from the decedent are generally not counted as income to you, so you do not pay federal income tax on those monies. If the monies you inherit later earn interest or income for you, then of course you will report that income as you do any other type of income.

Real and personal property are inherited at a "step up" in basis. This means that if the decedent purchased an item that is now worth more than when he purchased it, the beneficiary will inherit the property at its fair market value as of the decedent's date of death. For example, suppose the decedent bought stock for $20,000 and it is now worth $50,000, the beneficiary takes a step-up in basis of $30,000; i.e., he inherits the stock at the $50,000 value. If the beneficiary sells the stock for $50,000, he pays no Capital Gains tax. If the beneficiary holds onto the stock and later sells it for $60,000, the beneficiary will pay a Capital Gains tax only on the $10,000 increase in value since the decedent's death.

The step-up in basis is particularly important to spouses in a **Community Property** state such as Washington. Community Property includes all the earnings of either or both spouses; and all of the property they acquire after marriage, with the exception of property inherited by one spouse through gift or inheritance. During their lifetime each spouse owns half of their Community Property. When one spouse dies all of the Community Property that they hold jointly gets a step-up in basis. The surviving spouse then owns the property 100% with a basis equal to the market value as of the date of death (RCW 64.28.040).

SPOUSE — SELLING THE HOME

In the tough "ole days" the IRS used to allow Capital Gains Tax exclusion (up to $125,000) on the sale of one's homestead (the principal residence). A person had to be 55 or older to take advantage of the exclusion, and it was a once-in-a-lifetime tax break. If a married couple sold their home and took the exclusion it was "used up" and no longer available to either partner.

In these, the good times, the IRS allows you to sell your homestead and up to $250,000 ($500,000 for a married couple) of the home-sale profit is tax free (IRC Section 121(b) 3). There is no limit on the number of times you can use the exclusion, provided you own and live in the homestead at least two years of the last five years prior to the sale (26 U.S.C. 121). If, under the old law, the decedent and his spouse used their "once in a lifetime" homestead tax exclusion, with this new law, the surviving spouse can sell the homestead and once again take advantage of a tax break.

BENEFICIARY OF A
WASHINGTON HOMESTEAD

Special Situation

There is a ***Homestead Tax Exemption*** for people over the age of 61 who have owned their residence for over two years. If the decedent was entitled to this Exemption, then the surviving spouse need only be 57 or more as of the date of death to continue with the Exemption. The amount of the Exemption is based on income, so the surviving spouse needs to apply for his/her own Exemption.

People who are permanently disabled are also entitled to a Homestead Tax Exemption. A new owner who is disabled or at least 61 years old, as of December 31st of the year of the transfer, can apply to the County Assessor for his own Exemption. Application can be made at any time during the year. If approved, it will take affect the following year.

If the decedent was receiving a Homestead Tax Exemption, then whether or not the new owner intends to occupy the property as his homestead, the County Assessor needs to be notified of the change of ownership. This is done by filing the appropriate Department of Revenue form (RCW 84.36.381, 84.36.383, 84.36.385).

You can get information about tax forms and the telephone number and address of each County Assessor from the Internet.

WASHINGTON STATE DEPARTMENT OF REVENUE
http://dor.wa.gov

AN ESTATE TAX FOR THE WEALTHY

Both the federal and state government have the right to impose an *Estate Tax* on property transferred to a beneficiary as a result of the death. All the property owned as of the date of death becomes the decedent's *Taxable Estate*. This includes *real property* (residential lots, condominiums, etc.) and *personal property* (life insurance policies, cars, business interests, securities, IRA accounts, etc.). It includes property held in the decedent's name alone, as well as property that he held jointly or in Trust. It also includes gifts given by the decedent during his lifetime that exceeded $10,000 per person, per year. This *Annual Gift Tax Exclusion* is now based on the cost of living index. It is currently $11,000 (IRS 2503(b)).

For most of us, this is not a concern because no federal Estate Tax need be paid unless the decedent's Taxable Estate exceeds the federal *Estate Tax Exclusion* amount. That value is currently one and a half million dollars and is scheduled to go even higher:

YEAR	ESTATE TAX EXCLUSION AMOUNT
2004-2005	$1,500,000
2006-2008	$2,000,000
2009	$3,500,000

In 2010 the federal Estate Tax is scheduled to be phased out altogether; however in 2011, the Estate Tax will be reinstated unless lawmakers change the tax law once again.

There is an unlimited marital tax deduction for property transferred to the surviving spouse; so in most cases, no Estate tax need be paid if the decedent was married. Regardless of whether taxes are due, federal and state Estate tax returns must be filed whenever the decedent's Estate exceeds the federal Estate Tax Exclusion Amount in effect as of his date of death.

THE UN-UNIFIED GIFT TAX

Up until the year 2002, if you gave someone more than $10,000 in any given year you had to report that gift to the IRS. As explaineed, the Annual Gift Tax Exclusion is now adjusted for the cost of living and is currently $11,000. The IRS keeps a running count of amounts that you give over the Annual Gift Tax Exclusion. Although you are required to report the gift, no tax need be paid unless that running total is more than the federal Estate Tax Exclusion amount. If your running total does not exceed that amount during your lifetime, once you die, the cumulative value of gifts reported to the IRS will be added to your Taxable Estate.

Up until the change in the tax law in 2001, the Gift and Estate tax were unified. No Gift Tax needed to be paid unless the total value of the taxable gifts exceeded the federal Estate Tax Exclusion amount. That changes in 2004. In 2004, the Estate Tax Exclusion amount goes up to $1,500,000, but the amount for the Gift Tax Exclusion remains at $1,000,000, so they are no longer unified.

To summarize:
If you make a gift to anyone that is greater than the Annual Gift Tax Exclusion for that year, you must report the gift to the IRS. The IRS will keep count of values that you gave in excess of the Annual Gift Tax Exclusion. In 2004, and thereafter, if that sum exceeds $1,000,000, you will pay a Gift Tax on any amount that you give that is over the Annual Gift Tax Exclusion.

The Estate Tax is scheduled to be repealed in 2010, but not the Gift Tax.

The current federal Estate tax is scheduled to be phased out in the year 2010, but a new Capital Gains Tax is scheduled for 2010 that may prove even more costly than the Estate Tax. The new Capital Gains Tax is related to the way inherited property is evaluated by the federal government. Real and personal property is inherited at a "step up" in basis, meaning that if the decedent's property has increased in value from the time he acquired it, the beneficiary will inherit the property at its fair market value as of the decedent's date of death. For example, if the decedent bought stock for $20,000 and it is worth $50,000 as of his date of death, the beneficiary will take a step-up in basis of $30,000; i.e. the beneficiary inherits the stock at the current $50,000 value. If the beneficiary sells the stock for $50,000, he pays no Capital Gains Tax. If the beneficiary holds onto the stock and later sells it for $60,000, the beneficiary will pay a Capital Gains Tax only on the $10,000 increase in value since the decedent's death.

Up to 2009, there is no limit to the amount a beneficiary can take as a step-up in basis. But in 2010 caps are set in place. The decedent's Estate will be allowed a 1.3 million dollar step-up in basis, plus another 3 million for property passing to the surviving spouse. The new law could result in a significant Capital Gains Tax that the beneficiary must pay. For example, suppose in 2010 you inherit a business from your father that he purchased for $100,000 and it is now worth 2 million dollars. There is a capital gain of 1.9 million dollars, but you are allowed a step-up in basis of only 1.3 million. If you sell it for 2 million dollars, $600,000 of your inheritance will be subject to a Capital Gains Tax.

DECEDENT WITH A TRUST

If the decedent was the Grantor (or Settlor) of a Trust, then he was probably managing the Trust as Trustee during his lifetime. The Trust document should name a *Successor Trustee* to manage the Trust now that the Grantor is deceased. The Trust document may instruct the Successor Trustee to make certain gifts once the Grantor dies or the Trust document may direct the Successor Trustee to hold money in trust for a beneficiary of the Trust.

 **LAWYER**

IF YOU ARE SUCCESSOR TRUSTEE

If you are the Successor Trustee then in addition to following the terms of the Trust, you are required to obey all of the laws of the state of Washington relating to the administration of the Trust. For example, before making a significant non-routine transaction, you must notify certain Trust beneficiaries at least 20 days before making the transfer. A significant transaction is the sale of Trust property that represents 25% or more of the assets of the Trust (RCW 11.100.140). You should consult with an attorney experienced in Estate Planning to help you administer the Trust according to the law and without any liability to yourself.

IF YOU ARE A BENEFICIARY

If you are a beneficiary of the Trust, then you need to obtain a copy of the Trust provisions that apply to you and learn how the Trust will be administered now that the Grantor or Settlor is deceased. Most Trust documents are written in "legalese," so you may want to employ your own attorney to review the Trust, and explain your rights under that Trust.

NOTIFYING THE BUSINESS COMMUNITY

People and companies who were doing business with the decedent need to be notified of his death. This includes utility companies, banks, brokerage firms and any company that insured the decedent.

NOTIFY INSURANCE COMPANIES

Examine the decedent's financial records to determine the name and telephone number of all of the companies that insured the decedent or his property. This includes real property insurance, motor vehicle insurance, health insurance and life insurance.

MOTOR VEHICLE INSURANCE

Locate the insurance policy for all motor vehicles owed by the decedent (car, truck, snowmobile, boat, airplane) and notify the insurance company of the death. Determine how long insurance coverage continues after the death. Ask the insurance agent to explain what things are covered under the policy. Is the motor vehicle covered for all types of casualty (theft, accident, vandalism, etc.) or is coverage limited in some way?

If you can continue coverage, then determine when the next insurance payment is due. Hopefully, the car will be sold or transferred to a beneficiary before that date, but if not, you need to arrange for sufficient insurance coverage during the Probate procedure.

LIFE INSURANCE COMPANIES

If the decedent had life insurance, you need to locate the policy and notify the company of his death. Call each life insurance company and ask what they require in order to forward the insurance proceeds to the beneficiary. Most companies will ask you to send them the original policy and a certified copy of the death certificate. Send the original policy by certified mail or any of the overnight services that require a signed receipt for the package. Make a copy of the original policy for your records before mailing the original policy to the company.

BANK ACCOUNT LIFE INSURANCE

Many banks, credit unions, savings and loan associations provide life insurance at no cost to the primary owner of the account. Such insurance is often overlooked when settling the decedent's affairs. Even though the amounts are generally small ($1,000 to $5,000), they can add up if the decedent had several accounts in different places. Contact each financial institution to determine whether such insurance is provided by the company.

IF YOU CANNOT LOCATE THE POLICY

If you know that the decedent was insured, but you cannot locate the insurance policy, you can contact the company and request a copy of the policy. A tougher question is how to locate the policy if you can't find the policy and do not know the name of the insurance company. The American Council of Life Insurers offers suggestions that you may find helpful at the Missing Policy Inquiry page of their Web site.

AMERICAN COUNCIL OF LIFE INSURERS
http://www.acli.com

IF YOU CANNOT LOCATE THE COMPANY

If you cannot locate the insurance company it may be doing business under another name or it may no longer be doing business in Washington. Each state has a branch of government that regulates insurance companies doing business in that state. If you are having difficulty locating the insurance company call the Department of Insurance in the state where the policy was purchased and ask for assistance in locating the company. In Washington, that number is (360) 753-3613.

EAGLE PUBLISHING COMPANY OF BOCA has the telephone number for the Department of Insurance for each state at their Web site.

EAGLE PUBLISHING COMPANY OF BOCA
http://www.eaglepublishing.com

 ACCIDENTAL DEATH

If the decedent died as a result of an accident, then check for all possible sources of accident insurance coverage including his homeowner's policy. Some credit card companies provide accident insurance as part of their contract with their card holders.

If the decedent died in an automobile accident, check to see whether he was covered by any type of travel insurance, such as rental car insurance. If he belonged to an automobile club, such as AAA, then check whether he had accident insurance as part of his club membership.

HOMEOWNER'S INSURANCE

If the decedent owned his own home, then check whether there is sufficient insurance coverage on the property. The decedent may have neglected to increase his insurance as the property appreciated in value. If you think the property may be vacant for some period of time, then it is important to have vandalism coverage included in the policy. Once the property is sold, or transferred to the proper beneficiary, you can have the policy discontinued or transferred to the new owner. The decedent's Estate should receive a rebate for the unused portion of the premium.

MORTGAGE INSURANCE

If the decedent had a mortgage on any parcel of real estate that he owned, he might have arranged with his lender for an insurance policy that pays off the mortgage balance in the event of his death. Look at the closing statement to see if there was a charge for mortgage insurance. Also check with the lender to determine if such a policy was purchased.

If the decedent was the sole owner of the property, then the beneficiary of that property needs to make arrangements with the lender to either continue making payments of the mortgage or to refinance the property.

NOTIFY THE HOMEOWNER'S ASSOCIATION

If the decedent owned a condominium or a residence regulated by a homeowner's association, then the association will need to be notified of the death. Once the property is transferred to the proper beneficiary, he/she will need to contact the association to learn of the rules and regulations regarding ownership and to arrange to have notices of dues and assessments forwarded to the new owner.

WORK RELATED INSURANCE

If the decedent was employed, then check his records for information about work related benefits. He may have survivor benefits from a group life insurance plan and/or a company retirement plan. Also check with the employer about company benefits. If the decedent belonged to a union, then contact them to determine whether there are any union benefits.

The decedent may have belonged to a professional, fraternal or social organization such as the local Chamber of Commerce, a Veteran's organization, the Kiwanis, AARP, the Rotary Club, etc. If he belonged to any such organization, check to see whether the organization provided any type of insurance coverage.

 *Special Situation* **BUSINESS OWNED BY DECEDENT**

If the decedent owned his own company or was a partner in a company, he may have purchased "key man" insurance. Key man insurance is a policy designed to protect the company should a valuable employee become disabled or die. Benefits are paid to the company to compensate the company for the loss of someone who is essential to the continuation of the business. Ultimately, the policy benefits those who inherit the business.

If the decedent had an ownership interest in an ongoing business (sole proprietor, shareholder or partner), there may be a shareholder's or partnership agreement requiring the company to purchase the decedent's share of the business. The Personal Representative or his attorney needs to investigate to see if there was a Key man insurance policy and/or such purchase agreement.

CORPORATE OWNER OR REGISTERED AGENT

Special Situation

If the decedent was the sole owner of a corporation, i.e., the company stock was in his name only, then there may need to be a Probate procedure in order to transfer the company to the new owner.

If the decedent was the sole officer and/or Registered Agent of the company then the Corporations Division of the Washington Secretary of State needs to be notified of the identity of the new officers and Registered Agent as soon as is practicable (RCW 23B.05.010, 23B.05.020).

Forms to provide notice of the change of officers, directors and Registered Agent can be obtained by writing or calling the Corporation Division of the Washington Secretary of State at (360) 753-7115 or writing to:

Washington State Office of the Secretary of State
Corporations Division
801 Capitol Way S
P.O. Box 40234
Olympia, WA 98504-0234

If you were not actively involved in running the business, then you might request a status report of the company. The report will show whether filing fees are current and will identify the officers and directors of the company. You can get information about Washington corporations from the Web site of Washington's Secretary of State.

WASHINGTON SECRETARY OF STATE
http://www.secstate.wa.gov/corps/

NOTIFY ADVERTISERS

Probably the last in the world to learn of the decedent's death is the direct mail advertiser. Advertisers are nothing if not tenacious. It is not uncommon for advertisements to be mailed to the decedent for more than ten years after the death. It is not because the advertiser is trying to sell something to the decedent, but rather the people who prepare (and sell) mailing lists do not know that the person is dead.

Those who sell mailing lists may not be motivated to update the list because of the cost of doing the necessary research; and maybe even because the price of the mailing list is often based on the number of people on the list. Even those who compose their own list may decide it is less costly to mail to everyone, than take the time (and money) to update the list.

If it gives you pleasure to think of advertisers spending substantial sums for nothing, then that is what you should do (nothing). But for those of you who wince each time you see another piece of mail addressed to the decedent, you can write to the Direct Marketing Association and ask that the name be deleted from all mailing lists:

Mail Preference Service
Direct Marketing Association
P.O. Box 9008
Farmingdale, NY 11735

You will need to give them the decedent's complete address, including zip code and every name variation that the decedent may have used; for example:

Mr. Theodore James Jones
Ted Jones   Ted J. Jones
T. J. Jones   T. James Jones, etc.

HEALTH INSURANCE

The Health Insurance carrier probably knows of the death, but it is a good idea to contact them to determine what coverage the decedent had under that insurance plan. If you cannot find the original policy, have the insurance company send you a copy of the policy so that you can determine whether medical treatment given to the decedent before his death was covered by that policy.

 *Special Situation* → **DECEDENT ON MEDICARE**

If the decedent was covered by Medicare, you do not need to notify anyone, but you do need to know what things were covered by Medicare so that you can determine what medical bills are (or are not) covered by Medicare.

The government publication MEDICARE AND YOU (Publication No. CMS-11007) explains what things are covered under Medicare. You can get the publication by writing to:

U.S. Dept. of Health and Human Services
Centers for Medicare and Medicaid Services
7500 Security Boulevard
Baltimore, MD 21244-1850

You can also find the publication on the Internet.

 MEDICARE WEB SITE
http://www.medicare.gov

SPOUSE   HEALTH INSURANCE FOR THE SURVIVING SPOUSE

If the spouse of the decedent is insured under Medicare, then the death does not affect the surviving spouse's coverage. If the surviving spouse was not covered by Medicare but has her own health insurance that also covered the decedent, then the spouse needs to notify the employer of the death because this may affect the cost of the plan to the employer and/or the spouse.

If the spouse was covered under the decedent's policy then he/she needs to arrange for new coverage. There are state and federal laws that ensure continued coverage under the decedent's policy for a period of time depending on whether the decedent's employer falls under federal or state regulation.

If the decedent was employed by a federally regulated company (usually a company with at least twenty employees), then under the Consolidated Omnibus Budget Reconciliation Act ("COBRA") the employer must make the company health plan available to the surviving spouse and any dependent child of the decedent for at least 36 months. The employer is required to give notice to the surviving spouse that the spouse and/or dependent child have the right to continue coverage under the decedent's health plan. The spouse and/or child have 60 days from the date of death or 60 days after the employer sends notice (whichever is later) to tell the employer whether the surviving spouse and child wish to continue with the health insurance plan (29 USC 18 Sec. 1162, 1163).

The only problem with continued coverage may be the cost. Before the death, the employer may have been paying some percentage of the premium. The employer has no such duty after the death unless there was some employment agreement stating otherwise. Under COBRA, the employer may charge the spouse for the full cost of the plan plus a 2% administrative fee. If you have a question about your coverage under COBRA, you can call the U.S. Department of Labor ("DOL") at (800) 998-7542 and ask for the number of your local DOL office. You can also ask that they send you their publication HEALTH BENEFITS UNDER COBRA; or you can visit their Web site for more information.

 U. S. DEPARTMENT OF LABOR
http://www.dol.gov/dol/pwba

CONTINUED COVERAGE UNDER WASHINGTON LAW

Every insurer that issues a group disability insurance policy covering hospital or medical expenses must allow the spouse and dependent child the right to continue the group benefits for a period of time after the policy holder is no longer covered under that policy. The policy must provide that when coverage ends, the spouse and dependent child be given the opportunity to obtain a conversion policy. To get the conversion policy the spouse must submit a written application and the initial premium payment within 31 days after the group coverage terminates (RCW 48.21.250, 48.21.260).

Whether or not the insurance coverage falls under COBRA, it is important that the surviving spouse contact the employer, and the insurer, to learn of details of converting to a new policy as soon as is practical after the death.

✍ CHANGE BENEFICIARIES ✍

If the decedent was someone you named as beneficiary of your insurance policy, Will or Trust, brokerage account or pension plan, then you may need to name another beneficiary in his place:

INSURANCE POLICY ✍

If you named the decedent as the primary beneficiary of your life insurance policy, then check to see whether you named a contingent (alternate) beneficiary in the event that the decedent did not survive you. If not, then you need to contact the insurance company and name a new beneficiary. If you did name a contingent beneficiary, then that person is now your primary beneficiary and you need to consider whether you wish to name a new contingent beneficiary at this time.

HEALTH INSURANCE POLICY ✍

If the decedent was covered under your health insurance policy, then your employer and the health insurer need to be notified of the death because this may affect the cost of the plan to you and/or your employer.

WILL OR TRUST ✍

Most Wills provide for a contingent beneficiary in the event that the person named as beneficiary dies first. If you named the decedent as your beneficiary, then check to see whether you named an alternate beneficiary. If not, you need to have your attorney revise your Will and name a new beneficiary.

Similarly, if you are the Grantor or Settlor of a Trust and the decedent was one of the beneficiaries of your Trust, then check the Trust document to see if you named an alternate beneficiary. If not, contact your attorney to prepare an amendment to the Trust, naming a new beneficiary.

BANK AND SECURITIES ACCOUNTS ✐

If the decedent was a beneficiary of your bank or securities account, or if the decedent was a joint owner of your bank account or securities account, then it is important to contact the financial institution and tell them about the death. You may wish to arrange for a new beneficiary or joint owner at this time.

PENSION PLANS ✐

If the decedent was a beneficiary under your pension plan, then you need to notify them of his death and name a new beneficiary. Many pension plans require that you notify them within a set period of time (usually 30 days) so it is important to notify them as soon as you are able. If the decedent was a beneficiary of your Individual Retirement Account ("IRA") or of your Qualified Retirement Plan ("QRP") and you did not provide for an alternate beneficiary, then you need to name someone at this time.

Before you choose an alternate beneficiary, it is important that you understand all of the options available to you. Not an easy task. There are many complex government regulations relating to IRA and QRP accounts. Even if you believe you understood your options when you set up your account, the federal government often changes those options.

Your choice of beneficiary might impact the amount of money you can withdraw each month, so it is important to consult with your accountant or tax attorney or financial planner, before you make your election.

NOTIFY CREDIT CARD COMPANIES

You need to notify the decedent's credit card companies of the death. If you can find the contract with the credit card company check to see whether the decedent had credit card insurance. If the decedent had credit card insurance, then the balance of the account is now paid in full. If you cannot find the contract contact the company and get a copy of the contract along with a statement of the balance due as of the date of death.

DESTROY DECEDENT'S CREDIT CARDS

You need to destroy all of the decedent's credit cards. If you hold a credit card jointly with the decedent, then it is important to waste no time in closing that account and opening another in your name only.

That's something Barbara knows from hard experience. She and Hank never married but they did live together for several years before he died from liver disease. Hank came from a well to do family so he had enough money to support himself and Barbara during his long illness. Hank put Barbara on all of his credit card accounts so that she could purchase things when he became too ill to go shopping with her. After the funeral, Barbara had a gathering of friends and family at their apartment.

Barbara was so preoccupied with her loss that she never noticed that Hank's credit cards were missing until the bills started coming in.

Barbara did not know who ran up the bills on Hank's credit cards during the month following his death. It was obvious that Hank's signature had been forged — but who forged it? One credit card company suspected that it might have been Barbara herself just to get out of paying the bill by claiming that the card was stolen.

Because the cards were held jointly, Barbara became liable to either pay the charges or prove that she did not make the purchases. She was able to clear her credit record but it took several months and she had to employ an attorney to do so.

NOTIFYING OTHER CREDITORS

It is the job of the person appointed as Personal Representative to notify the decedent's creditors of the death so that the creditor is given an opportunity to come forward and present a claim for monies owed. The attorney for the Personal Representative usually takes care of the notice procedure, but see page 101 for an explanation of what is involved.

If no Probate procedure is necessary, then the next of kin can notify the creditors of the death, but before doing so, read Chapter 4: WHAT BILLS NEED TO BE PAID? That chapter explains what bills need to be paid and who is responsible to pay them.

Before any bill can be paid you need to know whether the decedent left any assets that could be used to pay those debts. The next chapter explains how to identify, and then locate all of the property owned by the decedent.

Locating the Assets 3

It is important to locate the financial records of the decedent and then carefully examine those records. Even the partner of a long-term marriage should conduct a thorough search because the surviving spouse may be unaware of all that was owned (or owed) by the decedent.

It is not unusual for a surviving spouse to be surprised when learning of the decedent's business transactions, especially in those cases where the decedent had control of family finances. One such example is that of Sam and Henrietta. They married just as soon as Sam was discharged from the army after World War II. During their marriage, Sam handled all of the finances giving Henrietta just enough money to run the household.

Every now and again Henrietta would think of getting a job. She longed to have her own source of income and some economic independence. Each time she brought up the subject Sam would loudly object. He had no patience for this new "woman's lib" thing. Sam said he got married to have a real wife — one who would cook his meals and keep house for him.

Henrietta was not the arguing type. She rationalized, saying that Sam had a delicate stomach and dust allergies. He needed her to prepare his special meals and keep an immaculate house for him. Besides, Sam had a good job with a major cruise line and he needed her to accompany him on his frequent business trips.

Once Sam retired, he was even more cautious in his spending habits. Henrietta seldom complained. She assumed the reason for his "thrift" was that they had little money and had to live on his pension.

They were married 52 years when Sam died at the age of 83. Henrietta was 81 at the time of his death. She was one very happy, very angry and very aged widow when she discovered that Sam left her with assets worth well over a million dollars!

LOCATING PERSONAL RECORDS

As you go through the papers of the decedent you may come across documents that indicate property ownership, such as bank registers, stock or bond certificates, insurance policies, brokerage account statements, etc. Place all evidence of ownership in a single place. You will need to contact the different companies in order to transfer title to the proper beneficiary. Chapter 5 explains how to identify the proper beneficiary of the decedent's property. Chapter 6 explains how to transfer the property to that beneficiary.

You may also need to produce evidence of the decedent's personal relationships, such as a marriage certificate, birth certificate, or naturalization papers, a Final Judgement of Divorce, military personnel records, etc. If you cannot locate his marriage certificate or birth certificate, you can get a certified copy of those records from the Vital Records office in the state where the event took place. See page 26 for the address and telephone number of Washington's Center for Health Statistics You can find the location and telephone number for other states by calling information or from the Internet by using your favorite search engine to locate Vital Records.

For deceased veterans, you can obtain a copy of his military record by writing to:

The National Personnel Records Center
Military Personnel Records
9700 Page Avenue
St. Louis, MO   63132-5100

They will send you form SF 180 to complete. You can get the form from the Internet at http://www.cem.va.gov or from the National Archives and Records Administration Fax-On-Demand system. Dial (301) 713-6905 and request document number 2255.

COLLECT AND IDENTIFY KEYS

The decedent may have kept his records in a safe deposit box, so you may find that your first job is to locate the keys to the box. As you go through the personal effects of the decedent, collect and identify all the keys that you find. If you come across an unidentified key, it could be a key to a post office box (private or federal) or a safe deposit box located in a bank or in a private vault company. You will need to determine whether that key opens a box that contains property belonging to the decedent or whether the key is to a box no longer in use. Some ways to investigate are as follows:

☑ CHECK BUSINESS RECORDS

If the decedent kept receipts, look through those items to see if he paid for the rental of a post office or safe deposit box. Also, look at his check register to see if he wrote a check to the Postmaster or to any safe deposit or vault company. Look at his bank statements to see if there is any bank charge for a safe deposit box. Some banks bill separately for safe deposit boxes so check with all of the banks in which the decedent had an account to determine if he had a box with that bank.

☑ CHECK THE KEY TYPE

If you cannot identify the key take the key to all of the local locksmiths and ask whether anyone can identify the type of facility that uses such keys. If that doesn't work, then go to each bank, post office and private safe deposit box company located where the decedent shopped, worked or frequented and ask whether they use the type of key that you found.

☑ CHECK THE MAIL

Check the mail over the next several months to see if the decedent receives a statement requesting payment for the next year's rental of a post office or safe deposit box.

FORWARD THE DECEDENT'S MAIL

You may find evidence of a brokerage account, bank account, or safe deposit box by examining correspondence addressed to the decedent. If the decedent was living alone, then have the mail forwarded to the person he named as Personal Representative or Executor of his Will. If the decedent did not leave a Will then the mail should be forwarded to his next of kin. Call the Postmaster and ask him/her to send you the necessary forms to make the change. Request that the mail be forwarded for the longest period allowed by law (currently one year).

The decedent may have been renting a post office box at his local post office branch or perhaps at the branch closest to where he did his banking. Ask the Postmaster to help you determine whether the decedent was renting a post office box. If so, then you need to locate the key to the box so that you can collect the decedent's mail.

 **LOST POST OFFICE BOX KEY**

If the decedent had a post office box and you cannot locate the key, then contact the local postmaster and ask him/her what documentation is needed for you to gain possession of the mail in that box. As before, you will ask the Postmaster to have all future mail addressed to that box, forwarded to the Personal Representative, or if there is no Will, then to the decedent's next of kin.

WHAT TO DO WITH CHECKS

You may receive checks in the mail made out to the decedent. Social security checks, pension checks and annuity checks issued after the date of death need to be returned to the sender. (See pages 30 and 32 of this book.) Other checks need to be deposited. If a Probate procedure is necessary, then the Personal Representative will open a Probate Estate account and the checks should be deposited to that account.

If no Probate procedure is necessary, then the checks can be deposited to any account held in the name of the decedent. The decedent is not here to endorse the check, but you can deposit it to his account by writing his bank account number on the back of the check and printing beneath it "FOR DEPOSIT ONLY."

The bank will accept such an endorsement and deposit the check into the decedent's account. If the check is significant in value and/or the decedent had different accounts accessible to different people, then there needs to be cooperation and a sense of fair play. If not, the dollar gain may not nearly offset the emotional turmoil. That was the case with Gail. Her father made her a joint owner of his checking account to assist in paying his bills. He had macular degeneration and it was increasingly difficult for him to see. The father also had a savings account that was in his name only.

Gail's brother, Ken, had a good paying job in Florida. Even though he lived at a distance, Ken, his wife and two children always spent the spring break with his father. Gail's good cooking added to the festivities. Each winter their father enjoyed leaving the cold behind him to spend a few weeks in the warmth of his family and the Florida sun.

One year, the father treated himself to a first class ticket to Miami. It cost several hundred dollars. Just before the departure date, the father had a heart attack and died. Gail called the airline to cancel the ticket. They refunded the money in a check made out to her father. She deposited the check to the joint account.

As part of the Probate procedure, the money in the father's savings account was divided equally between Ken and his sister. Ken wondered what happened to the money from the airline tickets.

Gail explained "He paid for the tickets from the joint account, so I deposited the money back to that account. "

"Aren't you going to give me half?"

"Dad meant for me to have whatever was in that joint account. If he wanted you to have half of the money, he would have made you joint owner as well."

Ken didn't see it that way: "That refund was part of Dad's Probate Estate. It should have been deposited to his savings account to be divided equally between us. Are you going to force me to argue this in court?"

Gail finally agreed to split the money with Ken, but the damage was done.

Gail complains that the holidays are lonely since her father died.

LOCATING FINANCIAL RECORDS

To locate the decedent's assets you need to find evidence of what he owned and where those assets are located. His financial records should lead you to the location of all of his assets so your first job is to locate those records. The best place to start the search is in the decedent's home. Many people keep their financial records in a single place but it is important to check the entire house to be sure you did not miss something.

CHECK THE COMPUTER
Don't overlook that computer sitting silently in the corner. It may hold the decedent's check register and all of the decedent's financial records. The computer may be programmed to protect information. If you cannot access the decedent's records, you may need to employ a computer technician or computer consultant who will be able to print out all of the information on the hard drive of the computer. You can find such a technician or consultant by looking in the telephone book under:

COMPUTER SUPPORT SERVICES or
COMPUTER SYSTEM DESIGNS & CONSULTANTS.

LOCATE TITLE TO MOTOR VEHICLE

The Washington State Department of Licensing is in charge of issuing certificates of title for motor vehicles, boats that are at least 16' in length and mobile homes. In the state of Washington, if monies are owed on a motor vehicle, the lender takes possession of the original certificate of title until the loan is paid. If you cannot find the original certificate of title, then it is either lost or monies are owed on the car and the lienholder has the original title.

You can check to see if there is a lienholder by calling (360) 902-3770. You will need to identify the vehicle by giving them the license plate number or the Vehicle Identification Number. You can find the Vehicle Identification Number on the dashboard of the car or on the car registration.

THE LEASED CAR

When you call the Department of Licensing you may find that the car is leased and not owned by the decedent. If such is the case, then you should contact the lessor and get a copy of the lease agreement. Once you have the lease agreement, check to see whether the decedent had life insurance as part of the agreement. If he did, the lease may now be paid in full and the beneficiary of the car should be able to use the car for the remainder of the leasing period, or take title to the car, whichever option is available under the lease agreement. The Personal Representative (or the beneficiary) can send the death certificate to the leasing company with a copy of the contract and a letter requesting that the transfer be made.

If the lease is not paid in full upon the decedent's death, arrangements will need to be made to satisfy the terms of the lease agreement. See Chapter 6 for information about transferring a leased car.

LOST TITLE

If there is no lease or lienholder and you cannot locate the title to the car, then in order to transfer the car, you will need to complete a form called AN AFFIDAVIT IN LIEU OF TITLE. The Department of Licensing will give you the Affidavit when the car is being transferred to the new owner. See Chapter 6 for information about transferring the motor vehicle.

LOCATE TITLE TO AIRCRAFT

If the decedent owned an aircraft, then you should find a certificate of title to the aircraft. The Civil Aviation Registry of the Federal Aviation Administration ("FAA") contains all of the ownership and security documents that have been filed with the FAA. If you cannot locate title to the aircraft you can contact the Civil Aviation Registry. They do not perform title searches, however they can give you a list of title search companies. If you wish to perform the title search yourself you can call the Aircraft Registration Branch at (405) 954-3116 for more information or you can visit the FAA Web site.

 THE FEDERAL AVIATION ADMINISTRATION
http://www2.faa.gov

In addition to locating the title you need to find the registration to the aircraft. Washingto statute requires that all aircraft be registered with the Washington State Department of Transportation (RCW 47.68.230, 47.68.250) (If you cannot locate the registration to the aircraft, you can call the Department of Transportation at (800) 552-0666 or write to them at:

Washington State Department of Transportation
Aviation Division
3704 172nd Street NE, Suite K2
PO Box 3367
Arlington, WA   98223-3367

You can get information about registering the airplane by visiting the Aviation Division section of the Department of Transportation Web site.

 DEPARTMENT OF TRANSPORTATION
http://www.wsdot.wa.gov/Aviation/

LOCATE CONTRACTS

If the decedent belonged to a health club or gym, he may have prepaid for the year. Look for the club contract. It will give the terms of the agreement. If you cannot locate the contract then contact the company for a copy of the agreement. If the contract was prepaid, then determine whether the agreement provides for a refund for the unused portion; or an assignment of the unused membership to the decedent's heir.

SERVICE CONTRACT
Many people purchase appliance service contracts to have their appliances serviced in the event that an appliance should need repair. If the decedent had a security system then he may have had a service contract with a company to monitor the system and contact the police in the event of a break-in.

If the decedent had a service contract, then you need to locate it and determine whether it can be assigned to the new owner of the property. If the contract is assignable, the new owner can reimburse the decedent's Estate for the unused portion. If the contract cannot be assigned, then once the property is transferred, try to obtain a refund for the unused portion of the contract.

LOCATE OUT OF STATE ACCOUNTS

If the decedent had out of state bank or brokerage accounts, then you might be able to locate them if they mail the decedent monthly or quarterly statements. Not all institutions do so, but all institutions are required to send out an IRS tax form 1099 each year giving the amount of interest earned on that account. Once the forms come in, you will learn the location of all of the decedent's active accounts.

DECEDENT'S RESIDENTIAL LEASE

If the decedent was renting his residence, then he may have a written lease agreement. It is important to locate the lease because the decedent's Estate may be responsible for payments under the lease. If you cannot locate the lease, then ask the landlord for a copy. If the landlord reports that there was no written lease, then verify that the decedent was on a month to month basis and then work out a mutually agreeable time in which to vacate the premises.

If a written lease is in effect, then determine the end of the lease period, and whether there was a security deposit. Ask whether the landlord will agree to cancel the lease on the condition that the property is left in good condition. If the landlord says that the Estate is responsible to pay the balance of the lease, then it is prudent to have an attorney review the lease to determine what rights and responsibilities remain now that the tenant is deceased.

☎ LAWYER

DECEDENT'S ONGOING BUSINESS

If the decedent was the sole owner of a business, or if he owned a partnership interest in a business, the Personal Representative needs to contact the company accountant to obtain the company's business records. If there is a company attorney, then the attorney may be able to assist in obtaining the records. If you are a beneficiary of the Estate, consider consulting with your own attorney to determine what rights and responsibilities you may have in the business.

COLLECT TAX RECORDS

You will need to file the decedent's final federal income tax return so you need to collect all of his tax records for the past 3 years. If you cannot locate his prior tax records, check his personal telephone book and/or his personal bank register to see if he employed someone to prepare his taxes. If you can locate his tax preparer, then he/she should have a copy of those records.

If you are unable to locate the decedent's federal tax returns then they can be obtained from the IRS. The IRS will send copies of the decedent's tax filings to anyone who has a *fiduciary relationship* with the decedent. The IRS considers the following people to be a fiduciary:

➢ the person appointed as the Personal Representative of the decedent's Estate

➢ the successor Trustee of the decedent's Trust

➢ if the person died *intestate* (without a Will), then whoever is legally entitled to possession of the decedent's property (see Chapter 5 for Washington's Laws of Descent)

The fiduciary can receive copies of the decedent's tax filings by notifying IRS that he/she is acting in a fiduciary capacity, and then requesting the copies.

To notify the IRS of the fiduciary capacity file Form 56:
    NOTICE CONCERNING FIDUCIARY RELATIONSHIP
To request the copies, file IRS Form 4506:
    REQUEST FOR COPY OR TRANSCRIPT OF TAX FORM

Your accountant can file these forms for you or you can obtain the forms from the IRS by calling (800) 829-3676 or you can download them from the Internet.

 IRS FORMS WEB SITE
http://www.irs.gov/forms_pubs/forms

COLLECT DEEDS

Collect deeds to all of the property owned by the decedent. In addition to the deed, look for other documents associated with title to the land, such as a mortgage. You may come across a Title Insurance policy. The new owner can turn in that policy and receive a discount toward the purchase new title insurance, so it is important to keep the policy together with the deed. Instead of a title insurance policy you may find an **Abstract of Title**. An Abstract of Title is a summary of the documents or facts appearing on the public record which affect title to the property. The Abstract will need to be updated once the property is transferred.

Many people keep deeds in a safe deposit box. If you cannot find the deed in the decedent's home, then you need to determine whether he had a safe deposit box and if so, you need to examine the contents of the box. See the end of this chapter for information about how to access the decedent's safe deposit box.

If you know that the decedent owned real property (lot, residence, condominium) but you cannot find the deed, then contact the office of the County Auditor or the Recorder's Office in the county where the property is located. The Auditor can provide you with a copy of the last recorded deed. You will need to identify the parcel of land by giving the Auditor the legal description of the land or its tax identification number. You can find this information on the last tax bill sent to the decedent. If you cannot locate the last tax bill, you can call the Auditor's office and they will give you the information. Title companies with offices in the county where the property is located, often provide copies of deeds as a customer service. The title company may be able to locate the deed with just the street address of the property.

| Special Situation | LOCATING THE OUT OF STATE DEED |

You need to locate the deed and any related document (Abstract of Title, Title Insurance policy, recorded condominium approval, etc.) to out of state property owned by the decedent.

THE LOST OUT OF STATE DEED

If you know the decedent owned out of state real property, but you cannot find the deed to the property, you can use the same procedure just described, namely, you can check with the recording department in the county where the property is located. In some states the Clerk of the Circuit Court is in charge of the recording department. In other states it may be the County Recorder or Registrar of Deeds. The Clerk in the recording department should be able to give you a copy of the last recorded deed.

If you do not know where the property is located, you may need to wait for the next tax bill. In many states the tax bill contains its legal description, or tax identification number.

Many states index the property by the name of the current owner of the property, so if you know the county where the property is located, you should be able to find the deed by giving the decedent's name to the Clerk.

FINDING LOST/ ABANDONED PROPERTY

If the decedent was forgetful, he may have money in a lost bank account or abandoned safe deposit box. Property that is unclaimed is turned over the to Washington State Department of Revenue after a period of time as set by Washington law. For most items it is 5 years, but that time period varies depending on the item:

- ⧖ 1 year for unclaimed wages
- ⧖ 1 year after a utility deposit or refund is payable
- ⧖ 5 years from last activity on a bank account
- ⧖ 5 years from the issuing date for a money order
- ⧖ 15 years from the issuing date of a travelers check

(RCW 63.29.020, 63.29.040, 63.29.050, 63.29.080, 63.29.150).

The Department of Revenue attempts to contact the last known owner through letters and advertisements in a newspaper in the county of the owner's last known address. Within 5 years of receiving the item the Department will convert tangible property to cash through public auction. The Department will give the net proceeds to the owner (or his heir) if a valid claim is made after the sale (RCW 63.29.180, 63.29.220, 63.29.240).

You can determine whether there is a record identifying the decedent as the owner of abandoned property by calling in-state (800) 435-2429; out of state (360) 664-8746 or by writing to Washington Department of Revenue
Unclaimed Property Section
P.O. Box 448
Olympia, WA   98507-0448

or by visiting their Web site.

 WASHINGTON UNCLAIMED PROPERTY DIVISION
http://www.wa.gov/dor/wador

CLAIMS FOR DECEDENT VICTIMS OF HOLOCAUST

The New York State Banking Department has a special Claims Processing Office for Holocaust survivors or their heirs. The office processes claims for Swiss bank accounts that were dormant since the end of World War II. If the decedent was a victim of the Holocaust, you can get information about money that may be due to the decedent's Estate by calling (800) 695-3318.

In Washington, Holocaust survivors or their heirs can get information about how to recover proceeds from insurance policies that were improperly denied by calling (888) 606-9622 or writing to:

Washington State Holocaust Survivors Assistance Office
Insurance Building, P.O. Box 40255
Olympia, WA 98504-0255

or visiting the State Insurance Web site.

 Washington State Insurance Commissioner
http://insurance.wa.gov/holocaust

CLAIMS FOR IRS TAX REFUNDS

The IRS reports that some 90,000 tax refund checks representing 67.4 million dollars were returned to them as being not deliverable. They keep the information on file and will forward the full amount once they locate the taxpayer. You can determine whether they are holding a check for the decedent by calling the IRS at (800) 829-1040.

CLAIMS IN OTHER STATES

Each state has an agency or department that is responsible for handling lost, abandoned or unclaimed property located within that state. If the decedent had residences in other states, then call the UNCLAIMED or ABANDONED PROPERTY department of the state Treasury to see if the decedent has unclaimed property in that state. Eagle Publishing Company has all of these telephone numbers at their Web site. http://www.eaglepublishing.com.

THE LOST PENSION

The decedent may be entitled to benefits under a pension plan of a prior employer. If the decedent worked for an employer for any significant period of time, say 5 years or more, then you need to check with the company benefit representative to determine whether any pension funds are payable. If you are unable to locate the former employer, then it could be that the company moved or merged with another company. There are several ways to track down the company, starting with the Secretary of State to learn of the company's current status (see page 47).

CONTACT THE UNION If company workers belonged to a union, you can contact the union and they may be able to help you locate the company; or tell you what happened to the pension funds.

CONTACT SOCIAL SECURITY The Social Security Administration has the decedent's work record and the employer identification number for each of his employers. The Personal Representative should be able to get that information by calling the Social Security Administration at (800) 772-1213. Using the employer identification number you might be able to determine whether the pension fund has been taken over by another company.

RESEARCH THE INTERNET Pension Benefit Guaranty Corporation operates an online search tool for those employees whose pension plans were taken over by regulators because the company filed for bankruptcy, or because the company dissolved the plan. All you need do is go to the pension search prompt at their Web site.

 PENSION BENEFIT GUARANTY CORPORATION
http://www.pbgc.gov

 **LAWYER**

THE PROBATE OF OUT OF STATE PROPERTY

If the decedent had his residence in Washington and owned property in another state, then you may need to conduct the initial Probate in Washington and an *ancillary* (secondary) Probate in the other state. If the decedent had his residence in another state and owned property in Washington, then it may need to be the other way around; namely, you may need to conduct the initial Probate in the other state.

If you are going to be Personal Representative, and the decedent owned property in another state or was a resident of another state, then before depositing the Will with the Court you should consult with an experienced Probate attorney in each state to determine where the initial Probate should be conducted. Convenience is important, but there are other things your need to consider:

COST OF PROBATE Ask each attorney whether the location of the initial Probate procedure will have an effect the total cost of Probate.

WHO INHERITS THE INTESTATE ESTATE Intestate laws vary significantly state to state. If the decedent died without a Will, it is important to determine whether the location of the inital Probate procedure will change the amount each heir will inherit.

ESTATE/INHERITANCE TAXES You need to determine whether the location of the inital procedure will have an impact on the amount of taxes that need to be paid.

FILING THE WILL

Anyone who has possession of the decedent's Will is required to deliver the Will either to the Executor named in the Will or the Clerk of the Superior Court within 30 days of learning of the death. An Executor who has custody of the Will has 40 days to file it with the Court (RCW 11.20.010). The Will should be filed in the county where the decedent lived. If owned property in Washington, but did not live here, then you need to deposit the Will with the Superior Court in the county where the property is located.

The Clerk will accept an original Will only and not a copy, so it is important to hand carry the original document to the Clerk. If you are the Executor of the Will, you can give it to your attorney to file with the court as part of the Probate procedure. Make a copy of the Will for your own records before delivering it to the Superior Court or to your attorney.

Special Situation   WILL DRAFTED IN ANOTHER
                                        STATE OR COUNTRY

A Will that conforms to the laws of the state or country where it was prepared and signed can be admitted to Probate the same as any Washington Will. A Will drafted in another language will need to be translated into English before it can be admitted into Probate.

A Will that has been admitted to Probate in another state can be used to distribute property here in Washington. To begin the ancillary Probate, a certified copy of the Will and of the original Probate record will need to be presented to the Washington Probate court (RCW 11.12.020, 11.12.090).

THE MISSING WILL

People tend to put off making a Will until they think they need to. For many, that need arises when they are elderly and/or seriously ill and have property that they want to leave to someone. It is uncommon for a young person to have a Will; but those who are aged, with significant assets, usually have one.

A survey conducted for the American Association of Retired Persons ("AARP") found that the probability of having a Will increases with age. Forty-four percent of those surveyed who were between the ages of 50 to 54 had a Will. This increased to 85% for those 80 and older. You can find details of the survey at the AARP Web site.

AARP WEB SITE
http://research.aarp.org

Those who make a Will, usually tell the person who they appoint as Executor of the existence of the Will. Chances are that someone in the decedent's circle of family and friends knows whether there is a Will. If you believe that the decedent had a Will but you cannot find it, then there are at least three places to check:

⇨ **THE CLERK OF THE SUPERIOR COURT**
Washington law requires that whoever has the original Will must deposit it with the Court within 30 days of the death. It is a good idea to check with the Clerk in the Superior court on the chance that someone found the Will and filed it with the Court.

⇨ THE DECEDENT'S ATTORNEY

Look at the decedent's checkbook for the past few years and see whether he paid any attorney fees. If you are able to locate the decedent's attorney, then call and inquire whether the attorney ever drafted a Will for the decedent, and if so, whether the attorney has the original Will in his possession.

If the attorney has the original Will, then ask the attorney to forward the Will to the Clerk of the Superior Court. Asking the attorney to forward the Will to the Court does not obligate you to employ the attorney should you later find that a Probate procedure is necessary.

⇨ THE SAFE DEPOSIT BOX

Many people keep their original Will in a safe deposit box. If you believe that the decedent had a Will but you cannot find it, then check to see if the decedent had a safe deposit box. If he did, you will need to gain entry to that box to see whether the Will is in the box. See the page 81 for an explanation of how to gain entry to the safe deposit box.

 **LAWYER**   A COPY BUT NO ORIGINAL

A person can revoke his Will simply by destroying or defacing it. If you have a copy of the Will and cannot find the original, the Court will presume that the decedent revoked that Will. You can ask the Judge to accept the copy into Probate, but you will need to prove to the Judge that the document is a true copy of the decedent's valid Will. You will also need to prove that the decedent had no intention of revoking that Will. These are not easy things to prove. You will need to employ an attorney experienced in Probate matters to present evidence to the Court.

There are certain circumstances that might justify admitting a copy of a Will into Probate. For example, suppose the decedent died in a house fire. If it can be proved that the original unrevoked Will was in the house, and if a true copy of the Will can be found, then the Court might decide to allow the copy into Probate (RCW 11.12.040, 11.20.070).

If you offer a copy of a Will and the Court does not allow it into Probate, then the decedent will be considered to have died without a Will, and his property distributed according to Washington's Laws of Descent and Distribution (see Page 119 for an explanation of the Law). This is case even if there is a prior valid Will. In the state of Washington, if a person revokes his Will by destroying it or by making a new Will, then regardless of what happens to the second Will, the first Will remains revoked. It cannot be revived just because a later Will cannot be found or has been revoked (RCW 11.12.080).

ACCESSING THE SAFE DEPOSIT BOX

When someone leases a safe deposit box, they sign an agreement with the bank, or lessor of the box, stating who can access the box. Two or more people can lease a safe deposit box so that each has free access to the box. Under Washington law, no matter what the leasing agreement with the bank states, there is no right of survivorship of the items within the box. If there are any items in the box that belong to the decedent, then those items will need to be given to the decedent's Personal Representative to be distributed as part of the Probate procedure (RCW 11.02.130).

The decedent could have leased a safe deposit box in his name only and give another person (his Agent) authority to enter the box. That authority could have been given as part of the lease agreement with the bank or in the form of a Power of Attorney given to the Agent by the lessee of the box. In Washington, the authority of an Agent to act under a Power of Attorney ends as soon as the Agent (or the bank) learns of the death. Once the bank learns of the death they will not allow the Agent, or even a joint tenant, to enter the box, for any reason, without Court authorization (RCW 11.94.010(1), 11.94.030).

In most cases that authorization is in the form of Letters issued by that Court giving the Personal Representative the right to take possession of all of the decedent's property. The Personal Representative can access the safe deposit box as soon as the Court signs his Letters.

It may be that no Probate procedure is necessary, but you still need to examine the contents of the box to determine whether there is anything of value in the box. In that case, you might ask your attorney to have the Court allow the attorney (as an officer of the Court) to take an inventory of the contents of the box. If anything of value is found, then a Personal Representative will need to be appointed to take possession of those items and distribute them according to the decedent's Will, or if no Will, then according to the Washington Laws of Descent (see Chapter 5).

There is no law that prevents an Agent or a joint tenant from removing the contents of the box, prior to the decedent's death. If the decedent had an Agent or a joint tenant, that person, may, as a precautionary measure, removed all of the items from the box when they learned that the lessee of the box was seriously ill. Before you seek Court authorization to examine the contents of the box, you need to check with that Agent, or joint tenant, to determine whether anything remains in the box.

Once you have located all of the decedent's property you may think the next step is to determine who gets to inherit that property. But some of that property may be needed to pay monies owed by the decedent; so the next step is to determine what, if any, bills need to be paid. That is the topic of the next chapter.

What Bills Need To Be Paid?

The Personal Representative has the duty to be sure that all valid *claims against the Estate* (demands for payment) are paid. If the decedent had debts, but no money or property, then of course, there is no way to pay the claim. The only remaining question is whether anyone else is responsible to pay the decedent's debts. If the decedent was married, then the first person the creditor will look to, is the decedent's spouse. To understand the basis of this expectation, you need to know a bit of the history of our legal system.

Our laws are derived from the English Common Law. Under early English Common Law, a single woman had the right to own property in her own name and also the right to contract to buy or sell property; but when she married, her legal identity merged with her spouse. She could not hold property free from her husband's claim or control. She could no longer enter into a contract without her husband's permission.

Once married, a woman became financially dependent on her husband. He, in turn, became legally responsible to provide his wife with basic necessities — food, clothing, shelter and medical services. If anyone provided basic necessities to his wife, then, regardless of whether the husband agreed to be responsible for the debt, he became obliged to pay for them. This law was called the DOCTRINE OF NECESSARIES.

States in America departed from English Common Law by enacting a series of Married Women's Rights Acts giving a married woman the right to own property and to contract in her own name.

Over the years each state developed its own laws relating to spousal responsibility. Some states decided to make the Doctrine of Necessaries part of their state law. States such as New Jersey and Ohio decided to apply the Doctrine equally to both sexes, making the husband responsible to pay for his wife's necessities and the wife responsible to pay for her husband's necessities. Other states abolished the law altogether making neither partner responsible to pay for the necessaries of the other.

Washington is a Community Property state. Whether a spouse is responsible to pay for the other's necessities (or any other debt) depends on whether there is Community property available. *Community Property* is property acquired by either the husband or the wife while they are married and residents of Washington. This does not include things either party inherits or receives as a gift during the marriage. If the parties lived in another state during the course of their marriage, then property they acquired as a married couple in another state is called *Quasi-community Property* (RCW 26.16.220).

For simplicity, we will use the term *Community Property* to include the couple's Community Property and their Quasi-community Property.

Separate Property is anything owned by a spouse prior to marriage and anything acquired by a spouse during the marriage as a gift or an inheritance. Any profit or increase in value of Separate Property is also Separate Property. For example, if a husband owned rental property prior to his marriage, then any money he receives as rental is Separate Property. If the property appreciates in value, then that increase in value is also separate property (RCW 26.16.010, 26.16.020).

COMMUNITY DEBT vs. SEPARATE DEBT

To understand the concept of a Community debt, think of the family unit as being a small community; and their family property (anything the couple purchases after marriage) as their Community Property. Any money spent for the benefit of the family or to manage or care for their family property becomes a Community debt to be paid from their Community Property. All of the couple's Community Property is available to pay for a Community Debt.

Monies owed by one of the partners prior to the marriage is his own Separate Debt, to be paid from his own Separate Property. If there is not enough Separate Property to pay that debt, then the creditor can require that the debtor's half of the Community Property be used to pay the debt.

If either husband or wife agree to pay for something, then the creditor can require Separate Property be used to pay for the debt. For example, if a couple purchase a home, then the mortgage on the home is a Community debt. The lender may ask both husband and wife to sign the promissory note. Once they sign, the loan becomes a Separate Debt of the husband and a Separate Debt of the wife. If there is not enough Community Property available to pay for the loan, then the lender can require that the husband and wife use their own Separate Property to pay for that loan (RCW 11.10.030, 26.16.200, 26.16.230).

Anything that the decedent agreed to pay for, is his own Separate Debt. If the decedent did not own sufficient property to pay for his Separate Debt, then his creditors cannot require more than half of the Community Property be used to unless that debt was also a Community Debt (RCW 11.02.07, 26.16.250). This applies even if the reason for the debt was some wrongdoing. For example, suppose the decedent had an accident while driving drunk. If he caused injury to someone else and they get a judgment against the decedent, then that judgment must be paid from the decedent's Separate Property. Washington courts have held that if separate funds are insufficient, then up to 50% of the Community Property must be used to pay the judgment *(DeElche v. Jacobsen, 95 Wn.2d 237 (1980), 622 P.2d 835)*

 **LAWYER**   MUCH DEBT AND LITTLE COMMUNITY PROPERTY

The decedent could have come into the marriage with nothing and contributed little to the marriage. In such case, there may be little, if any, Community Property available to pay his debts. No doubt his creditors will not see things that way. The creditor might suspect that there is property held in the name of the surviving spouse that is really Community property. The creditor might ask the Court to order an accounting to determine whether any of the property held by the spouse is Community Property.

If the decedent left much debt, it is important for the surviving spouse to consult with a Probate attorney to determine what rights and responsibilities remain to the surviving spouse.

JOINT DEBTS

A *joint debt* is a debt that two or more people are responsible to pay. Usually the contract or promissory note states that the parties agree to *joint and several liability*, meaning they all agree to pay the debt and each of them agree to be personally responsible for the debt. A joint debt can also be in the form of monies owed by one person with payment guaranteed by another person. If the person who owes the money does not pay, then the *guarantor* (the person who guaranteed payment) is responsible to make payment.

If the decedent was single, then his hospital bills, nursing home bills, funeral expenses, legal fees to Probate the decedent's Estate are all debts of his Estate. They are not joint debts unless someone guaranteed payment for the monies owed.

If the decedent was married, then all of these bills are Community Debts. If the decedent agreed to pay for his hospital or nursing home bill, then it is also his own Separate debt and the Personal Representative can use the decedent's Probate Estate to pay for those bills. If there are insufficient funds in the Probate Estate, then all of the Community Property is available to pay for those debts. The surviving spouse is not required to use his/her Separate Property to pay for any of these debts (medical care, funeral expense, legal fee) unless the surviving spouse agreed to be liable for payment.

JOINT PROPERTY BUT NO JOINT DEBT

Suppose all of the decedent's property (bank accounts, real estate, etc.) is held jointly with a family member (not his spouse). If the joint owner of the property did not agree to pay monies owed by the decedent, can the creditor require that the decedent's share of the property be used to pay his debts?

The answer to this question is "Yes." Any creditor has two years to come forward and demand payment from the decedent's share of the joint property. The time period can be shortened if there is a Probate procedure. The Personal Representative can publish notice in a legal newspaper. If he does so, the creditor must come forward within 4 months from the first day of publication. If there are insufficient funds in the Probate Estate, the Personal Representative can require the joint property be used to pay the debts (RCW 11.10.040, 11.42.050).

If no Probate procedure is necessary and you have inherited substantially all of the decedent property either through joint ownership or even as a beneficiary of a Trust, you might consider giving notice yourself. You can do so by becoming a *Notice Agent*. A Notice Agent is someone authorized by the Probate Court to publish notice to creditors (RCW 11.42.010). Notice must be in the manner and form as required by statutes 11.42.020 and 11.42.030. The Probate clerk can provide you with the necessary information.

If properly done, the time allowed for a creditor is reduced from 2 years to 4 months, but there is also the risk of opening Pandora's box. Best to seek the counsel of your attorney to determine whether becoming a Notice Agent is the best thing to do in the given circumstances.

NO MONEY — NO PROPERTY

If the decedent owed money then the debt needs to be paid from assets owned by the decedent — which leads to the next question "Did the decedent have any money in his own name when he died?"

If the decedent died without any money or property in his name, then there is no money to pay any creditor. The only question that remains is whether anyone else is liable to pay those bills. The issue of payment most often arises in relation to services provided by nursing homes. When a person enters a nursing home, he is usually too ill to speak for himself or even sign his name. In such cases, the nursing home administrator will ask the spouse or a family member to sign a battery of papers on behalf of the patient before allowing the patient to enter the facility. Buried in that battery of papers may be a statement that the family member agrees to be responsible for payment to the nursing home. If the family member refuses to guarantee payment and the patient's finances are limited, then the facility may refuse to admit the patient.

Under the Federal Nursing Home Reform Law, a nursing home that accepts Medicare or Medicaid payments is prohibited from requiring a family member to guarantee payment as a condition of allowing the patient to enter that facility (USC Title 42 §1395I-3(c)(5)(A)(ii)). Nonetheless, it is common practice for a nursing home, to say in effect "Either someone agrees to pay for the patient's bill or you need to find a different facility."

Their position is understandable. Most nursing homes are business establishments and not charitable organizations. The nursing home must be paid for the services they provide or they soon will be out of business. For an insolvent patient, the solution to the problem is to have the patient admitted to a facility as a Medicaid patient.

But what if the decedent had some money when he entered the nursing home and you agreed to guarantee payment to the nursing home?

What if you feel that you were coerced into signing as a guarantor?

Are you now liable to pay the decedent's final nursing home bill if your family member died without funds?

An experienced Elder Law attorney will be able to answer these questions after examining the documents that you signed and the conditions under which the patient entered the nursing home.

PAYING THE DECEDENT'S BILLS

If the decedent's Estate is solvent, i.e., there is money available to pay his debts, then it is the job of the Personal Representative to do so. Once the Probate procedure begins, all of the decedent's creditors will be given an opportunity to come forward and produce evidence showing how much is owed.

If the decedent was married and no Probate procedure is necessary, and there is Community Property available, then the surviving spouse needs to make provision for paying bills they were both responsible to pay.

The spouse or the Personal Representative needs to look over each unpaid invoice and decide whether it is a valid bill. The problem with making that decision is that the decedent is not here to say whether he actually received the goods and services now being billed to his Estate.

That is especially the case for medical or nursing care bills. An example of improper billing brought to the attention of this author was that of a bill submitted for a physical examination of the decedent. The bill listed the date of the examination as July 10th, but the decedent died on July 9th. Other incorrect billings may not be as obvious, so each invoice needs to be carefully examined.

If the Personal Representative decides to challenge a bill, and is unable to settle the matter with the creditor, then the Court will decide whether the debt is valid and should be paid.

MEDICAL BILLS COVERED BY INSURANCE

If the decedent had health insurance you may receive an invoice stamped "THIS IS NOT A BILL." This means the health care provider has submitted the bill to the decedent's health insurance company and expects to be paid by them. If the decedent was receiving Medicare, you will receive a *Medicare Summary Notice* listing all of the services or supplies that were billed to Medicare for the prior 30 days. In some areas of the country, you can get a copy of the decedent's Medicare Summary Notice from the Internet: http://www.medicare.gov

Even though payment is not requested, it is important to verify that the bill is valid for two reasons:

➤ LATER LIABILITY

If the insurer refuses to pay the claim, the facility will seek payment from whoever is in possession of the decedent's property, and that may reduce the amount inherited by the beneficiaries.

➤ INCREASED HEALTH CARE COSTS

Regardless of whether the decedent was covered by a private health care insurer or Medicare, improper billing increases the cost of health insurance to all of us. Consumers pay high premiums for health coverage. We, as taxpayers, all share the cost of Medicare. If unnecessary or fraudulent billing is not checked, then ultimately, we all pay.

If you believe that you have come across a case of Medicare fraud, you can call the ANTI-FRAUD HOTLINE (800) 447-8477 and report the incident to the Office of the Inspector General of the United States Department of Health and Human Services.

HOW TO CHECK MEDICARE BILLING

The structure of Medicare has been changed giving people in some parts of the country, the option of staying with the *Original Medicare Plan* or choosing one of the *Medicare + Choice Plans*. Coverage differs depending on which plan is chosen. If the decedent was covered by Medicare, you need to determine whether he was covered under the Original Medicare Plan, or whether he chose a Medicare + Choice Plan. The publication *Medicare and You* explains coverage under the different options. See page 49 to obtain a copy of the booklet.

An important billing question is whether the health care provider agreed to accept Medicare *assignment*, meaning that they agreed to accept the Medicare-approved amount. If so, the patient is responsible for the coinsurance (usually 20% of the approved amount) and any deductible amount. Doctors and health care providers who do not accept assignment, are limited in the amount they can charge for a Medicare covered service. The highest they can charge is **15%** over the Medicare-approved amount. This *Limiting Charge* applies only to certain services and does not apply to supplies and equipment.

If all of this appears confusing, it is.

To check the decedent's Medicare billing, you first need to determine whether he was in the Original Medicare Plan or in one of the Medicare + Choice Plans. The *Medicare and You* booklet explains what is covered under the Original Medicare Plan. You will need a copy of the contract for the Medicare + Choice Plans to determine what is covered under that plan. Once you know what is covered, you need to determine whether the health care provider accepted assignment; and if not whether the Limiting Charge applies to the services provided. Finally if assignment is accepted or the Limiting Charge applies, you need to determine the Medicare-approved amount.

Special Situation	DENIAL OF MEDICARE COVERAGE

If the health care provider reports to you that service provided to the decedent are not covered by Medicare, or if the facility submits the bill to Medicare and Medicare refuses to pay, then check to see if you agree with that ruling by determining what services are covered under Medicare. See page 49 of this book for information about how to obtain a pamphlet that explains what medical treatments are covered under Medicare.

The Statewide Health Insurance Benefits Advisors ("SHIBA") is a free counseling program provided by the state of Washington for Medicare recipients. You can call them at (800) 397-4422 for a counselor nearest you who can answer specific questions that you may have. The National Council on the Aging has a Web site that can refer you to other state and federal agencies in your area that may be able to assist you.

 NATIONAL COUNCIL ON AGING
http://www.benefitscheckup.org

APPEALING THE DECISION

If you believe that the decedent was wrongly denied coverage, then you can appeal that decision. If want a local attorney to assist with your appeal, then you can call your local Bar Association to refer you to an attorney experienced in Medicare appeals. Some attorneys work *pro bono* (literally for the public good; i.e., without charge) but most charge to assist in an appeal. Federal statute 42 U.S.C. §406(a)(2)(A) limits the amount an attorney may charge for a successful Medicare appeal to 25% of the amount recovered or $4,000, whichever is less.

SOME THINGS ARE CREDITOR PROOF

Sometimes it happens that the decedent had money or property titled in his name only, but he also had a significant amount of debt. In such cases the beneficiaries may wonder whether they should go through a Probate procedure if there will be little, if anything, left after the creditors are paid. Before making the decision consider that some assets are protected under Washington law:

✧ LIFE INSURANCE PROCEEDS ✧

The proceeds of a life insurance policy (not an annuity) paid to the decedent's beneficiary (and not to the Estate of the decedent) are exempt from the claims of the decedent's creditors. The insurance proceeds are also exempt from the existing claims of the beneficiary's creditors at the time of receiving the proceeds of the policy.

The only exception to this creditor protection is the purchase of a policy to defraud creditors. For example, suppose the decedent owed a large sum of money and instead of paying the debt, he used that sum to purchase a life insurance policy. If the creditor can prove that the purpose of the purchase was to avoid paying the debt, then the money paid by the decedent for the policy, plus interest on that amount, will be paid to the creditor from the proceeds of the policy (RCW 48.18.410).

PROCEEDS PAYABLE TO SPOUSE

Proceeds payable to the decedent's spouse become the Separate Property of the spouse. Proceeds of a life insurance policy payable to one of the decedent's married parents, becomes their Community Property, unless the policy specifically states otherwise (RCW 48.18.440).

✧ GROUP LIFE INSURANCE PROCEEDS ✧

The proceeds of a group life insurance policy are exempt from the claims of creditors even if the policy is payable to the decedent's Estate. Specifically, if the decedent's life is insured under a group life insurance policy, and the decedent names his Estate as the beneficiary of the policy, then whoever inherits his Estate will take the proceeds of the policy free from the claims of the decedent's creditors. Of course the insured person could name anyone else as beneficiary of the policy, and that person will inherit the proceeds free of the claims of the decedent's creditors and the beneficiary's creditors as well (RCW 48.18.420).

✧ PENSION PLANS ✧

Pensions, retirement or disability allowances, death benefits, profit sharing or other retirement plans, including IRAs and Keogh accounts, are creditor proof. Monies received by a beneficiary of such plans are protected from the decedent's creditors with the exception of monies owed for child support or for taxes (RCW 6.15.020).

Income taxes are not usually paid when money is placed in a retirement plan, so taxes must be paid when the monies are withdrawn from the account regardless of whether the monies are withdrawn by the retiree or the person named as beneficiary of the retirement plan. If you inherit money from the decedent's pension, annuity or retirement allowance, you should consult with an accountant or an attorney knowledgeable in tax law to determine how much money needs to be set aside to pay for federal and state income taxes.

✦ THE HOMESTEAD EXEMPTION ✦

Up to $40,000 of real property used as a homestead is exempt from creditors claims. If the homestead consists of personal property such as a mobile home, then up to $15,000 is exempt from the claims of the owner's creditors. This exemption is limited. It is not available for mortgages, mechanic's liens, certain bankruptcy procedures, or back child support payments (RCW 6.13.010, 6.13.030, 6.13.080).

Once the homeowner dies, his spouse and/or children, are entitled to this exemption in the form of an award by the Probate Court which we shall refer to as the *Family Allowance*. If the homeowner is not survived by spouse or child, then this homestead exemption is lost and any creditor may require that the homestead be sold to pay for monies owed by the decedent.

✦ THE FAMILY ALLOWANCE ✦

The surviving spouse can *petition* (ask) the Probate Court for an award for basic maintenance and support during the Probate proceedings. If the decedent was survived by child(ren) who were not also children of the surviving spouse, then they can ask the Court to share in that Family Allowance. If there is no surviving spouse, then only the decedent's minor children (or their Guardian) can petition for a Family Allowance (RCW 11.54.010, 11.54.030, 11.54.070).

The basic award is equal to the Homestead Exemption, but the Court can increase or decease that award based on the facts of the case; i.e., the size of the Estate; the length of the marriage; what resources are available to the surviving spouse and children; whether the decedent made any provision for their care; how the rest of the beneficiaries will be affected by increasing the award, etc. (RCW 11.54.020, 11.54.040)

The Family Allowance can be paid from the decedent's Separate Property, or from his share of the Community property. The Family Allowance is exempt from the claims of creditors. The only items paid before the family allowance are the funeral expenses and the expenses of administration (Probate filing fees, publishing notice to creditors, attorney and Personal Representative fees, etc.)

Anytime within 18 months from the decedent's death the surviving spouse can ask the Court for the award. The award can be made by the Court whether or not any Probate procedure is necessary. If there is no Probate procedure, the spouse has 6 years from the date of death to make the request (RCW 11.54.010).

If you are entitled to a Family Allowance, it is important to consult with an attorney who will prepare the Petition and advise you about the different factors that the Court will consider when deciding how much should be paid and what assets should be used to make the payment.

✦ THERE IS A PRIORITY OF PAYMENT ✦

Next to consider is that not all Probate debts are equal. Washington statute establishes an order of priority for payment of claims made against the decedent's Estate:

CLASS 1: COST AND EXPENSES OF ADMINISTRATION

The cost of the Probate procedure, including filing fees, and fees charged by the Notice Agent and/or the Personal Representative and his attorney, must be satisfied before any other debt can be paid. If the decedent was married, then these expenses are charged proportionally against the decedent's Separate Property and against the Community Property. It could happen that there is little Separate Property. In that case, the Court may require that all of the Community property be available to pay for the cost of the Probate proceeding (RCW 11.10.030).

CLASS 2: REASONABLE FUNERAL EXPENSES

The reasonable expenses of the decedent's funeral are second in priority.

CLASS 3: MEDICAL EXPENSES

Third in line is payment for the reasonable and necessary medical expenses of the decedent's last illness.

CLASS 4: FAMILY ALLOWANCE

Once the cost of the administration and the funeral and medical expenses are paid, the Probate Court can award the surviving spouse and/or children a Family Allowance.

CLASS 5: WAGE CLAIMS

If within 60 days of his death the decedent employed someone and the employee is owed wages, then that claim is 5th in priority of payment.

CLASS 6: FEDERAL TAXES

If monies or taxes are owed by the decedent to the federal government, and the monies owed have preference under federal law, then these debts are 6th in line for payment.

CLASS 7: STATE TAXES

Monies owed to the state of Washington for debts and taxes are seventh in priority.

CLASS 8: SECURED DEBTS

If the decedent has a secured debt such as a mortgage on a house, or a car loan, or even a judgment lien on property owned by the decedent, then those debts are 8th in line for payment.

CLASS 9: ALL OTHER CLAIMS

There are no priorities within a given class. For example, suppose an unmarried decedent left enough money to pay for the Probate procedure, his funeral, with $20,000 left over. If there are no other debts, his beneficiaries will inherit the $20,000.

Suppose instead that he left a hospital bill of $30,000 and a doctor's bill of $10,000 (both Class 3 debts). The $20,000 will be prorated with the hospital getting $15,000 and the doctor getting $5,000. There will be nothing left to pay a family allowance or other claim. There will be nothing left for anyone to inherit (RCW 11.42.090, 11.76.150).

✦ THERE IS A STATUTE OF LIMITATIONS ✦

There are federal and state laws that set time periods for pursuing a claim. Anyone who wishes to take court action must do so within the time set by the given Statute of Limitation. For example, in Washington, the Statute of Limitation for bringing suit against someone for assault and battery is 2 years. It is 6 years to sue for monies owed under a rental agreement, and so on. There are exceptions to the rule, for example, if someone committed battery against the decedent, the 2 year Statute of Limitations is extended a year, so the Personal Representative has 3 years from the date of the injury to file suit. But in general, if someone files a claim against the decedent's Estate and the Statute of Limitation for that claim has passed, then the claim will be refused (RCW 4.16.040, 4.16.100, 4.16.200, 11.40.051).

There is a Statute of Limitations for a creditor to come forward and make a claim against the decedent's Estate for monies owed. The Personal Representative (or anyone who inherits the decedent's property) can publish notice of the death for three successive weeks in a legal newspaper. He can also mail notice to any of the decedent's known creditors. The creditor must file the claim within 30 days of receipt of the notice. If the creditor is not given written notice, then he has 4 months from the first day that notice was published in the newspaper to file a claim with the Clerk of the Superior Court.

No one is required to give notice. If none is given, then a creditor has two years from the date of death to file a claim against anyone in possession of the decedent's Estate (RCW 11.42.050).

 **LAWYER**

DECEDENT LEAVING CONSIDERABLE DEBT

If the decedent died leaving much debt and no property, then the solution is simple. No Probate, no one gets paid. But if the decedent had property and died owing a significant amount of money, his heirs may be tempted to wait the two years and begin Probate at that time. Such strategy may turn out to be more hassle than it is worth. Some creditors are tenacious and will use whatever legal strategy is available in order to be paid. For example, if no one starts a Probate procedure, after 40 days from the date of death a creditor can petition the Court to be appointed as Personal Representative of the Estate (RCW 11.28.120).

As we will see in Chapter 6, the Personal Representative has much authority when conducting the Probate. Family members may object to having a creditor as a Personal Representative, so there could be a court battle over who has priority to be appointed as Personal Representative. Court battles are expensive, emotionally as well as financially. Before you decide to wait out a creditor by postponing Probate, consult with an attorney experienced in Probate matters for an opinion about the best way to administer the Estate.

Medicaid is a program that provides medical and long term nursing care for people with low income and limited resources. The program is funded jointly by the federal and state government. Federal law requires the state to recover monies spent from the Estate of a Medicaid recipient who was 55 or older when the decedent received Medicaid assistance. The state will seek reimbursement for the cost of nursing home care or for home based care or for other community based services. Federal law prohibits any recovery of monies until the surviving spouse, and/or disabled child of the decedent are deceased (42 U.S.C. 1396(p)).

Even if the Medicaid recipient is single, there usually is no money to recover because to qualify for Medicaid in Washington, a person may not have more than $2,000 in assets. But sometimes it happens that a person on Medicaid dies and his Estate later receives money perhaps as part of a settlement of a lawsuit. In such case, a Probate procedure will be necessary. The Office of Financial Recovery of the Washington Department of Social and Health Services will file a claim against the Estate to recover monies spent for the benefit of the decedent (RCW 43.20B.090).

The Personal Representative is not required to give notice to the decedent's creditors; but he is required to send notice of the death, and the decedent's social security number, to the Office of Financial Recovery. This must be done regardless of whether the decedent ever received government assistance (RCW 11.28.237, 11.40.020).

MONIES OWED TO THE DECEDENT

Suppose you owed money to the decedent. Do you need to pay that debt now that he is dead? That depends on whether there is some written document that says the debt is forgiven once the decedent dies. For example, suppose the decedent lent you money to buy your home. If he left a Will saying that once he dies, your debt is forgiven, then you do not need to make any more payments. If you signed a promissory note and mortgage at the time you borrowed the money from the decedent, then the Personal Representative should sign the original promissory note "PAID IN FULL" and return the note to you. If the mortgage was recorded, then the Personal Representative should sign and record a satisfaction of mortgage.

If you owed the decedent money and there is no Will, or if there is a Will, and no mention of forgiving the debt, you still owe the money. Monies borrowed from the decedent and his spouse need to be repaid to the spouse. Monies borrowed from the decedent only, become an asset to the Estate of the decedent, meaning that you owe the money to the decedent's Estate. If you are one of the beneficiaries of the Estate, you can deduct the money from your inheritance.

For example, suppose your father left $70,000 in a bank account to be divided equally between you and your two brothers. If you owed your father $20,000, then your father's Estate is really worth $90,000. Instead of paying the $20,000, you can agree to receive $10,000 and have the $20,000 debt forgiven. Each of your brothers will then receive $30,000 in cash.

Who Are The Beneficiaries? 5

A question that comes up early on is who is entitled to the property of the decedent. To answer the question you first need to know how the property was titled (owned) as of the date of death.

There are three ways to own property. The decedent could have owned property jointly with another person; or in trust for another person; or the decedent could have owned property that was titled in his name only.

In general, upon the decedent's death:

Joint Property with right of survivorship
belongs to the surviving joint owner.

Trust Property belongs to the beneficiary
of the trust.

Property owned by the **decedent only** is inherited
by the beneficiaries named in the Will.
If there is no Will, then the property goes to his heirs
according to the Laws of Descent and Distribution

NOTE ⇨ If the decedent was married, then his
spouse may have rights in his property.

This chapter describes each type of ownership in detail.

PROPERTY HELD JOINTLY

Bank accounts, securities, motor vehicles, real property can all be owned in *Joint Tenancy* by two or more people. In Washington, property held in joint tenancy has a right of survivorship, meaning that if one joint tenant dies, the remaining tenant(s) own the property, automatically and without the need for any Probate procedure.

Unless a Joint Tenancy is indicated, property that is held by two or more people is presumed to be an *Interest In Common* or a *Tenancy-In-Common* meaning that there are no rights of survivorship. Should one of the owners die, the share of the property belonging to the decedent belongs to the decedent's Probate Estate, to be distributed according to the decedent's Will or according to Washington's Laws of Descent and Distribution. Property held by a married couple as an Interest In Common is presumed to be their Community Property. All of the couple's Community Property becomes part of the decedent's Probate Estate with half going to the decedent's surviving spouse and the other half distributed according to his Will or the Laws of Descent and Distribution (see Page 119 for an explanation of the law) (RCW 64.28.010, 64.28.020).

THE JOINT BANK ACCOUNT

A joint bank account can be set up with or without rights of survivorship. If there are rights of survivorship, then any sum on deposit in a joint account may be withdrawn by each owner of the account, regardless of whether the other owner(s) are incapacitated or deceased. If all of the joint owners of an account are deceased, then the account goes to the Estate of the last of the owners to die (RCW 30.22.050, 30.22.100).

If a joint account is held in two or more names and one owner dies, then the share owned by the decedent is divided equally between the surviving owners. Of course, either of the survivors can go to the bank and withdraw all of the funds in the account. With such an arrangement, the surviving owners need to cooperate with each other to divide the funds in the account fairly, and to keep in mind that there may be claims on those funds either by the decedent's creditors or his surviving spouse.

JOINTLY HELD SECURITIES

You can determine whether the decedent owns a security alone or jointly with another by examining the face of the stock certificate. If two names are printed on the certificate followed by a statement that the owners are "Joint Tenants With Rights of Survivorship ("JTWRS")," or simply as "Joint Tenants," then the surviving owner can either cash in the security or ask the company to issue a new certificate in the name of the surviving owner. Co-owners of US Bonds hold the bond as Joint Tenants. Should one co-owner die, the other owns it 100% (RCW 11.02.110, 11.04.230).

Each state has its own securities regulations. If a security held in two or more names was registered or purchased in another state, then you will need to contact the company to determine how the account was set up; i.e., with or without rights of survivorship. If the decedent held his securities in a brokerage account, then the name of the owner of that account is printed on the monthly or quarterly brokerage statement. Not all brokerage firms print the name of a joint owner on the brokerage statement, so you need to contact the firm to determine whether there is a surviving joint owner, or perhaps a beneficiary of the account. Request a copy of the contract that is the basis of the account. The contract will show when the account was opened and the terms of the brokerage account.

If the title to a motor vehicle is held in the name of the decedent and another person followed by "in Joint Tenancy" or "as Joint Tenants with right of survivorship," then the surviving Joint Tenant owns the car, 100%. Nothing need be done to establish the ownership, but it is a good idea to change title for insurance reasons. Should the surviving owner be involved in an accident, and title has officially been changed, then there is no question that the Estate of the decedent is in no way liable for the accident. Also, the surviving owner might be able to get a reduced insurance rate if there is only one person insured under the policy.

If you are the surviving owner, you can change title to your name only by taking a certified copy of the death certificate to your local Department of Licensing. It is a good idea to first call to determine the cost of issuing the new certificate and whether they will require any documentation other than the death certificate.

If title to the motor vehicle was held in the name of the decedent and another person as a Tenant In Common, then the decedent's "half" is distributed in the same manner as if the car were titled in his name only.

MOTOR VEHICLE IN DECEDENT'S NAME ONLY

If the decedent's car was in his name only and he left a Will, then the car goes to the beneficiaries named in the Will. If the decedent died without a Will, then the car goes to the next of kin as defined in Washington's Laws of Descent and Distribution. See Chapter 6 for an explanation of how to transfer title to the motor vehicle.

REAL PROPERTY HELD JOINTLY

The name of the owner of real property is printed on the face of the deed. To determine whether the decedent owned the property jointly with another person, you need to look at the last recorded deed. See page 70 if you cannot locate the deed.

> ## WARRANTY DEED
>
> The Grantor ROBERT TRAYNOR, a single man,
> for and in consideration of $10.00
> in hand paid, conveys and warrants to
> SUSAN CODY, a single person and
> HENRY TRAYNOR, a single person,
> as **JOINT TENANTS**
> the following described real estate
>
> . . .

Robert Traynor is the *Grantor* of the deed. That means he transferred the property to Susan Cody and Henry Traynor who are the *Grantees* and present owners of the property. They own the property as *Joint Tenants*, meaning that there are rights of survivorship. Should one of them die, the surviving joint tenant owns the property 100%.

Nothing need be done to establish the ownership, however the decedent's name remains on the deed (RCW 11.04.250). Should the surviving owner want to transfer the property, all he/she need do is keep a certified copy of the death certificate to present at closing to prove that there is just one owner.

▤ DEED WITH A LIFE ESTATE

A *Life Estate* interest in real property means that the person who owns the Life Estate has the right to the possession of the property until he/she dies. He can chose to live on the property, or he can rent it out and keep the income. You can identify a Life Estate interest by examining the face of the deed. If somewhere on the face of the deed you see the phrase RESERVING A LIFE ESTATE to the decedent, then the Grantee(s) now own the property. For example, suppose the granting paragraph of the deed reads:

The Grantor PETER REILLY, a single man, for and in consideration of $10 in hand paid conveys and warrants to
ROSE SMITH, a married woman, the following described real estate

. . .

RESERVING A LIFE ESTATE TO THE GRANTOR

Peter Reilly is the owner of the Life Estate. Rose Smith is the *Remainder Beneficiary* of the property. Rose has no right to occupy the property during Peter's lifetime, but once he dies, Rose will own the property 100%. She will be free to take possession of the property or transfer it, as she sees fit. As with a Joint Tenancy, nothing need be done to establish Rose's ownership of the property, however she needs to keep a certified copy of Peter's death certificate to produce at closing in the event that she wants to sell or transfer the property at a later date.

📃 DEED HELD AS TENANTS IN COMMON

If the Grantee of a deed identifies the decedent and another as TENANTS IN COMMON, then unless the deed says differently, each Tenant In Common owns an equal share. If the decedent owned property as a Tenant In Common, then his share goes to the beneficiary of his Will. If the decedent died without a Will, then the Washington Laws of Descent and Distribution determine who inherits the decedent's share. A Probate procedure may be necessary in order to transfer the decedent's share of the property to the new owner.

If the deed names two or more people as the Grantee and does not say whether they are "Joint Tenants" or "Joint Tenants With Survivorship" then they hold title as Tenants in Common (RCW 64.28.020).

 **LAWYER**   **THE AMBIGUOUS DEED**

Most deeds clearly state whether there are rights of survivorship. But some deeds can be read two ways. For example, suppose a woman deeds her home to herself and her two children as follows:
> Ruth White, Grantor, ... to Ruth White
> jointly with Ralph White and Susan Peters."

Did Ruth intend that they all be joint tenants? Or did she intend that if one of her children died first, then that child's share would go to the deceased child's Estate? Best to consult with an attorney if you have any question about how to interpret the deed.

▤ DEED HELD AS HUSBAND AND WIFE

If a married couple holds property as follows:

TODD AMES AND SUSAN AMES, JOINT TENANTS

then should one spouse dies, the surviving spouse owns the property 100%. As explained, no document need be recorded to establish the ownership of the surviving joint owner.

If Joint Tenancy is not clearly indicated, then the property is considered to be Tenancy-In-Common. For example, if the Grantees is identified as:

TODD AMES AND SUSAN AMES, husband and wife

the property is held as a Tenancy-In-Common.

The difference between a couple holding the property as a Joint Tenant or as a Tenant In Common relates only to the right of the surviving spouse to inherit the property. It does not change the fact that such property is con-sidered to be their Community Property (RCW 11.04.071, 64.28.020, 64.28.040).

If the couple own the property as Tenants-In-Common, the decedent's share of their Community Property is distributed according to his Will, or if he had a written **Community Property Agreement** with the surviving spouse, then according to that Agreement. See the next page for an explanation of the Community Property Agreement.

In the absence of a Will or Community Property Agreement, his share will be distributed according to Washington's Laws of Descent and Distribution.

THE COMMUNITY PROPERTY AGREEMENT

A husband and wife have the right to enter into a Community Property Agreement, so that upon the death of one, their Community Property goes to the surviving spouse. The Agreement can cover all the Community Property they presently own or may acquire in the future. It can cover all of their Community Property or as much of their Community Property as they agree to. In order for the Community Property Agreement to be effective to transfer property, it must be signed by both spouses, acknowledged in the presence of a Notary Public, and then recorded in the Office of the Auditor in the county where the property is located.

Once the Agreement is properly recorded, should one spouse dies, the other spouse has the right to take possession of the Community Property without the need for any Probate procedure. The Community Property Agreement only transfers Community Property. Probate proceedings may still be necessary to transfer Separate Property owned by the decedent. It may also be necessary for the surviving spouse to officially change title to the property. For example, if the Community Property Agreement gives the family car to the surviving spouse, but title to the family car is in the name of the decedent, then the surviving spouse will need to have the title changed (RCW 26.16.120).

And of course, the Community Property Agreement, has no affect on the rights of creditors. As explained on Pages 85 and 86, all of the decedent's Separate Property and half of all Community Property is available to pay the decedent's Separate Debts. All of the Community Property is available to pay a Community Debt regardless of whether that debt was incurred by the decedent or the surviving spouse.

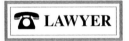 **LAWYER** OUT OF STATE DEED

This chapter relates only to property owned by the decedent in the state of Washington. If the decedent owned property in another state or country, the laws of that state or country, determine who inherits the property. Washington, being a Community Property, has laws relating to property held by a married couple that are very different from the laws of other states. In Washington, there is no right of survivorship unless the deed indicates that the couple hold the property as joint tenants.

In other states, such as Florida, there is a right of survivorship whenever the deed identifies the Grantees as being married. For example, a deed that identifies the couple as "husband and wife," or a deed that identifies the couple as "Tenants-by-Entirety" has rights of survivorship. When one party dies, the surviving spouse owns the property 100%.

If the decedent owned property in another state, it is important to consult with an attorney in that state to determine who owns the property now that the Grantee is dead.

 The above discussion on the different types of ownership of real property assumes that you are in possession of the most recent, valid deed. The decedent could have signed another, later deed. Before you come to a conclusion about who inherits the property it is advisable have a title company or an attorney do a title search to determine the owner of the property as of the decedent's date of death.

PROPERTY HELD IN TRUST

BANK/ SECURITY ACCOUNTS

If a bank account or security account is registered in the name of the decedent held "for the benefit of" or "in trust for" someone, then once the bank has a certified copy of the death certificate, the bank will turn over the account to the beneficiary. If the beneficiary is a minor the financial institution may require a Custodian be appointed to care for the funds until the child reaches the age of 21. If the funds exceed $30,000, the funds cannot be transferred without authorization of the Superior Court (RCW 11.114.070). Tranfers to minors are discussed in Chapter 7.

If the bank or security account is registered in the name of the decedent "as Trustee under a Trust agreement," that means the decedent was the Trustee of a Trust and the financial institution will turn over that account to the Successor Trustee of the Trust. Financial institutions usually require a copy of the Trust agreement when the account was opened, so they probably know the identity of the Successor Trustee, as well as the names of all of the beneficiaries of the Trust.

MOTOR VEHICLE

If the motor vehicle is held in the name of the decedent "as Trustee," then the motor vehicle continues to be Trust property. The Successor Trustee will need to contact the motor vehicle bureau to have title changed to that of the Successor Trustee. If the Trust Agreement directs the Successor Trustee to sell the car or to distribute that car to a beneficiary, then the Successor Trustee will need to arrange to have this done. See Chapter 6 for directions about how to transfer the car to a new owner.

REAL PROPERTY HELD IN TRUST

If the decedent had a trust and put property that he owned into the trust, then the deed may read something like this:

> The Grantor JOHN ZAMORA
> for and in consideration of $10 in hand paid
> convey and warrant to
> JOHN ZAMORA, **trustee of the**
> **JOHN ZAMORA TRUST AGREEMENT**
> DATED April 26, 2001,
> the following described real estate
> . . .

The death of the Trustee of a Trust does not change the ownership of the property. It remains in the Trust. The Trust document might say whether the person who takes John's place as Trustee (the Successor Trustee) should sell or keep the property or perhaps give it to a beneficiary. If no instruction is given, the Successor Trustee can use his discretion as to what to do with the property. If you are a beneficiary of the Trust and you are concerned about what the Successor Trustee will do with the property, then it is best to consult with your attorney to learn about your rights under that Trust.

WASHINGTON DEED OF TRUST

The Washington Deed of Trust is very different from the above described deed. The Deed of Trust is essentially a mortgage. The owner of the property places title to the property with a Trustee as security for payment of monies owed to the lender. If the debt is not paid, then the Trustee (after proper foreclosure on the property) will deliver title to the property to the Beneficiary of the Deed of Trust, namely the lender (RCW 61.24.005, 61.24.020).

If the decedent owned property that was in his name only (not jointly or in trust for someone), then some sort of Probate procedure will be necessary before the heirs can get possession of that property. Who is entitled to the decedent's Probate Estate depends on whether the decedent died with or without a Will. If the decedent died with a valid Will, then the beneficiaries of the decedent's property are identified in the Will.

If the decedent died without a Will, then his Probate Estate is distributed according to the Laws of Descent and Distribution (RCW 11.04.015). These laws determine who inherits the decedent's **Net Probate Estate** i.e., how much each heir receives once all the debts and the costs of the Probate procedure are paid.

The law recognizes the right of the family to inherit the decedent's property. The Laws of Descent covers all possible relationships beginning with the decedent's spouse. But before we investigate the law, we need to know who the state of Washington considers to be the surviving spouse.

Who Is The Spouse?
In this era of people challenging the concept of the family unit, those of a philosophical bent may ponder the meaning of marriage. Is it a union of two people in the eyes of God? Is it even a union? Maybe it is just an agreement between two people. The state does not concern itself with such things. If the decedent was a resident of the state of Washington and died without a Will, then his property is distributed according to the laws of the state; and the laws of the state of Washington determine whether the decedent was married.

MARRIED IN WASHINGTON

To be married in Washington means that a man and a woman have entered into a civil contract according to the laws of the state. Namely, they obtained a marriage license, solemnized the marriage by a state or religious ceremony, and then lived together as man and wife. Consent of a parent or guardian is required to issue a marriage license when either party is under 18. Consent of a Superior Court Judge is required for anyone under the age of 17 (RCW 26.04.010, 26.04.210).

Washington law specifically prohibits the issuance of a marriage license to those:
- ☒ who are currently married;
- ☒ who are the same sex;
- ☒ who are related closer than second cousin, regardless of whether the relationship is by whole or half blood (RCW 26.04.020)

THE COMMON LAW MARRIAGE

A common law marriage is one that has not been solemnized by ceremony. The couple agree to live as man and wife, and then publicly hold themselves out as being married. Common law marriages entered into in Washington are not considered to be a valid marriage. The surviving partner of such a union can inherit property as a beneficiary of the decedent's Will, but cannot inherit under the Washington's Laws of Descent and Distribution.

Marriages that are valid in another state are valid here — with the exception of marriages that are specifically prohibited (bigamy, same sex and marriage to a close relative). If an existing common law marriage is valid in another state and the couple move here, then the couple is considered to be married in Washington as well (*In Re Gallegher's Estate*, 35 Wn.2d 512 (1950). It is important to consult with an attorney if you have any question about the validity of the decedent's marriage.

WASHINGTON'S LAWS OF DESCENT

If the decedent died without a Will, then the state of Washington provides one for him in the form of the *Laws of Descent and Distribution.* These laws are also referred to as the *Laws of Intestate Succession*:

✧ SURVIVING SPOUSE ONLY

If the decedent was married and had no surviving *descendant* (children, grandchildren, etc.) or surviving parent, or descendant of his parents (brother, sister, nieces, nephews, great nieces, great nephews, etc.), then the spouse inherits all of the decedent's Estate. This includes all of the decedent's Separate Property, and the decedent's half of their Community Property. As explained on page 84, we are using the term "Community Property" to include any Quasi-Community Property that the couple may own.

✧ CHILD, NO SPOUSE

If the descendant was single and left descendants, then his Net Probate Estate is inherited by his descendants. If he had two or more children, all who survive him, then each child is entitled to an equal share of his Estate.

But suppose one of the decedent's children dies first. What happens to the share intended for the deceased child? In such case, the property is distributed *by Representation*. The definition of "by representation" is given in Washington statute 11.02.005. That definition appears on the next page.

If a decedent's Estate passes *by representation*, then

> "After first determining who, of those entitled to share in the Estate, are in the nearest degree of kinship, the Estate is divided into equal shares, the number of shares being the sum of the number of persons who survive the intestate who are in the nearest degree of kinship and the number of persons in the same degree of kinship who died before the intestate but who left issue surviving the intestate; each share of a deceased person in the nearest degree shall be divided among those of the deceased person's issue who survive the intestate and have no ancestor then living who is in the line of relationship between them and the intestate, those more remote in degree taking together the share which their ancestor would have taken had he or she survived the intestate.

If you understood the above definition and you are not a lawyer, then you missed your calling. For the rest of us (even lawyers) its a head-scratcher. Maybe the best way to explain "by representation" is by example.

Suppose the decedent was unmarried when he died, with 4 children, Ann, Barry, Carl, David. If he died intestate, then each of his children get 25% of his Net Probate Estate.

CHILD WITHOUT DESCENDANTS DIES BEFORE DECEDENT
If Ann dies before her father, leaving no descendants, then Barry, Carl and David divide the Estate between them. Each gets one third of the Net Probate Estate.

CHILDREN WITH DESCENDANTS DIES BEFORE DECEDENT
Suppose instead that only Carl and David survived their father. If Ann died leaving no children and Barry died leaving 2 children, then the Estate is divided into 3 shares — one for each surviving child (Carl and David) and one share for Barry's children, who split their share equally.

✧ SURVIVING SPOUSE AND CHILD

If the decedent had surviving descendants, the spouse gets all of the Community Property and half of the decedent's Separate Property. The other half goes to the decedent's descendants by Representation.

✧ SURVIVING SPOUSE, NO CHILD

If the decedent had no surviving descendants, but he had surviving parents , or descendants of his parents (i.e. the decedent's brother, sister, niece, nephew, etc.) the spouse gets all of the Community Property and 75% of the decedent's Separate Property. The remaining 25% is inherited by the decedent's parents. If only one parent is alive, then that parent gets the 25%. If neither parent is alive, then it goes to their descendants, by Representation; i.e., it goes to the decedent's brothers and sisters, by Representation.

✧ NO SPOUSE, NO CHILD

If there is no surviving spouse or descendant, then the entire Net Probate Estate goes to the decedent's parents, or the survivor of them. If no parent survives, then the Estate goes to their descendants (the decedent's brothers and sisters), by Representation. And if none of these, the grandparents inherit the Estate. If there are surviving maternal and paternal grandparents, the Estate is divided in half. The maternal grandparent (or grandparents) get 50% of the Estate and the paternal grandparent (or grandparents) get the other 50%.

If there are no surviving grandparents, then the entire Net Probate Estate goes to the descendants of the grandparents. If there are descendants on both the maternal and paternal side of the family, then the Estate is divided in half, with the maternal descendants taking 50% by representation and the paternal descendants taking 50% by representation (RCW 11.04.015)

THE STATE: HEIR OF LAST RESORT

As discussed previously, all unclaimed property goes to the state of Washington, so if a person dies without a Will and he has absolutely no next of kin, or he had a Will or Trust and no beneficiary can be found, then the state of Washington "inherits" the decedent's Probate Estate (RCW 11.08.140, 11.80.110).

 IT ISN'T ALL THAT SIMPLE

The explanation in this book of Washington's Laws of Descent is abridged. Even though you may now know more about the Laws of Descent than you ever wanted to know, there is much more to the law. For example, suppose someone with children (or descendants) marries and leaves all of his property to his spouse. Should the surviving spouse die without a Will, leaving absolutely no relatives of her own, then all of the property goes to the decedent's descendants, i.e., to the stepchildren of the deceased spouse, by representation (RCW 11.04.095).

Unless the descent is straight forward, with the decedent leaving a surviving spouse and/or children (all of whom survive him), it is best to consult with an attorney before you decide who is entitled to the decedent's intestate property.

WHO DIED FIRST?

Sometimes it happens that two family members die simultaneously, and no one knows who died first. For example, suppose a father and son die together in an airplane crash, how is the property distributed in that case?

Washington law provides for the orderly distribution of their property. Each is assumed to have survived the other and the property of each is distributed on that basis. The father's property is distributed as if he survived his son and the son's property is distributed as if he survived his father. For example, if the father named his son as beneficiary under his Will, then unless the Will makes a different provision, the son will be considered to have died before his father, and the Probate Estate distributed on that basis.

If the father and son owned property jointly, and they die simultaneously, the property will be divided with one half going to the Estate of the father and the other half going to the Estate of his son.

If the father had a life insurance policy with his son as beneficiary and a grandson as alternate beneficiary, then the proceeds of the policy will go to the grandson. (RCW 11.05.010, 11.05.020, 11.05.030, 11.05.040).

THE RIGHTS OF A CHILD

THE ADOPTED CHILD
An adopted child has the same rights to inherit property from his adoptive parents as does a natural child, even if the child was an adult when adopted. Once adopted, the child is no longer the heir of his natural parents (RCW 11.04.085, 26.33.260).

THE AFTERBORN CHILD
A child conceived prior to the decedent's death, and born after his death is considered to be living at the time of his death. The afterborn child has the same right to inherit as does any living child of the decedent (RCW 11.02.005).

THE NON-MARITAL CHILD
A child born out of wedlock has the right to inherit from his/her father, provided:

☑ the father married the mother and acknowledged the child as his own - or -

☑ the father was married to the mother and the child was born within 300 days from the termination of the marriage - or -

☑ the father took the child into his home as a minor and openly held out the child as his own - or -

☑ the father signed an affidavit, stating under oath that the child is his, and then filed it with the State Registrar of Vital Statistics - or -

☑ paternity was established through genetic testing. (RCW 11.04.081, 26.26.040).

If the decedent denied his paternity, then it will take a court procedure to establish (or disprove) paternity (RCW 26.26.060). If you want to establish paternity, then you need to consult with an attorney who is experienced in this type of litigation.

THE CHILD OF AN ASSISTED CONCEPTION

Medical technology has made important contributions to solving the problem of infertility. There are all sorts of solutions, from hormone replacement therapy, to sperm banks that provide donations anonymously, to frozen sperm and/or ova to be thawed and used at a later date, to women who serve as a Surrogate or gestation mother. Solving a set of medical problems has opened the door to a new set of legal problems. Used to be, the only question was "Who's the father?" Now it could well be "Who's the mother? Two major problems are the case of a woman who has an assisted conception without the knowledge and/or consent of her spouse; and the case of a child born to a Surrogate mother.

Under Washington law, a physician may not use artificial insemination to impregnate a married woman unless both she and her spouse give written consent. The physician is required to file the agreement with the Registrar of Vital Statistics, where it is kept confidential and in a sealed file. Once the child is born, the father is listed on the birth certificate as the child's natural father.

A child born to parents using any other form of assisted conception has the same rights as a child conceived the old fashioned way. It is presumed that the father consented to the assisted conception procedure. If such is not the case, and the husband is not the father of the child, he can petition the court to terminate his parental rights and responsibilities (RCW 26.26.060). If the husband is successful, the child will not be able to inherit from the husband, nor his family.

THE SURROGATE PARENTAGE CONTRACT

A Surrogate mother is a woman who agrees to become impregnated and then give up the child for adoption to the intended parents. The usual arrangement is the artificial insemination of the Surrogate mother using the sperm of the intended father. But there can be other arrangements — anything from no donation by the intended parents to the donation of a fertilized egg cell from the intended parents (making them biological parents of the child). And there can be all kind of problems with enforcing the agreement, from the Surrogate mother deciding not to allow the adoption, to one (or both) of the intended parents deciding not to adopt after all.

Some states, such as Virginia, allow a couple to contract with a woman to have their baby. The court supervises the contract and if all goes well, issues a birth certificate to the intended parents after the birth. Other states, such as Michigan, strictly prohibit Surrogate Parentage contracts.

Washington allows a Surrogate Parentage contract, provided no money is paid other than for medical expenses and attorney's fees; and provided that the Surrogate mother is not a minor, or mentally retarded. If there is a dispute after the child is born, the child will remain with whoever has physical custody until a Judge of the Superior Court decides what is in the child's best interest. If there is no dispute, the parties must still bring the matter before the Superior Court so that the intended parents can legally adopt the child (RCW 26.26.220, 26.26.230, 26.26.260).

Anyone who is found to have wilfully and unlawfully caused the death of the decedent, or who acted as an accomplice in the crime (the "killer") is prohibited from profiting from the crime. Property that the killer would have inherited as a beneficiary of the decedent's Will or according to the Laws of Descent and Distribution will be distributed as if the killer died before the decedent (RCW 11.84.010, 11.84.030, 11.84.040).

If the killer is a beneficiary of the decedent's life insurance policy, then whoever is named as alternate beneficiary will get the proceeds. If there is no alternate beneficiary, then the proceeds go to the decedent's Probate Estate (RCW 11.84.100).

The decedent's half of property held jointly by the decedent and his killer will not descend to the killer. The decedent's half will go to the decedent's Estate. The killer's half will go to the decedent's Estate once the killer dies. The killer can ask the Court to divide the property. If the Court agrees the killer will continue to own his/her half of the joint property (RCW 11.84.050).

NO AWARD FOR KILLER

The Court will not make an award of a Family Allowance to a spouse or child who has participated in the willful and unlawful killing of the decedent (RCW 11.54.030).

WHEN TO CHALLENGE THE WILL

It is not uncommon for a family member to be unhappy with the way the decedent willed his property. If you are tempted to challenge a Will, first consider whether the Will is valid under Washington law.

In Washington, a Will is presumed to be valid if at the time the decedent made the Will:

➢ he was of sound mind, and

➢ he was at least 18 years of age (RCW 11.12.010).

A Will can be challenged at any time within 4 months from the date the Will was accepted (or rejected) by the Court. You can ask the Court to disregard the Will if you can prove that at the time the Will was signed, the decedent was of unsound mind, meaning that:

⇨ he didn't know what he was doing
(namely making a Will) - or -

⇨ he didn't understand how much property he had - or -

⇨ he didn't remember or understand his relationship to his family members or how they would be affected by his Will.

Proving that the decedent was of unsound mind is a difficult task because Washington courts have ruled that if a Will looks rational and is legal in its form, then it is presumed that the Will maker was mentally capable of making the Will (*In Re: Estate of Nelson*, 85 Wn.2d 602 (1975)). But you can still challenge the Will if you can prove that the decedent was pressured or persuaded to sign the Will by someone close to him. To prove that he was being unduly influenced, you will need to show that he did not act intelligently, voluntarily, and of his own free will, but rather according to the will and purpose of that person.

THE UNWITNESSED WILL

Washington law requires that the Will be in writing and signed by the person who is making the Will in the presence of two witnesses. The witnesses to the Will should be people who have no interest in the Will (except the Witness can be a creditor of the Will maker).

If the decedent's Will was witnessed by someone who is a beneficiary of the Will, then unless there are two other, disinterested witnesses to the Will, it is presumed that there was undue influence, if not fraud. Even if it is found that such was not the case, the gift to that witness cannot be more than what the witness would have received if the decedent died without a Will (RCW 11.12.160).

The first step in the Probate procedure is to have the Probate court determine whether the Will presented is valid. There should be no problem having the Will accepted into Probate if the Will was signed in the presence of at least two disinterested witnesses. But suppose the decedent wrote out a Will in his own hand and signed it with no one present? Such a Will is called a *holographic Will.* Many states, including Washington, refuse to accept a holographic Will into Probate. The problem with a holographic Will, in this or any other state, is its authenticity. Because no one saw the decedent sign the Will, it is hard to determine whether the Will was written by the decedent or is a forgery.

THE VERBAL WILL

Picture a death bed scene. The elderly gentleman is surrounded by several family members. In a whisper, just audible enough to be heard, he says:

"Even though I am a wealthy man, I never got around to making a Will. You all have been good to me, but I did want my entire fortune to go to my nephew, Robert. He has been like a son to me. "

Do you think Robert can inherit his Uncle's Estate?

Not in Washington unless:
⇨ Someone writes down his uncles's wishes, and
⇨ The uncle acknowledges that this is his Will, and
⇨ The uncle tells someone to sign the Will for him, and that person does so in his presence and in the presence of two people who sign as witnesses (RCW 11.12.020).

Considering that the uncle's relatives will probably inherit the fortune under Washington's Laws of Descent and Distribution, it is doubtful that Robert is in danger of becoming wealthy at any time in the near future.

THE THOUSAND DOLLAR EXCEPTION
Washington law does allow a gift of personal property of $1,000 in value or less to be given as a death bed wish, provided:
⇨ the gift was reduced to writing; and
⇨ within 6 months of making the gift at least two witnesses testify that the decedent said that this was his Will; and
⇨ the surviving spouse and other heirs are notified of the gift and given an opportunity to contest the gift (RCW 11.12.025).

THE WILL THAT IS CONTRARY TO LAW

Sometimes a person who is of sound mind makes a Will, but that Will has the effect of giving a spouse or a minor child less than is required under Washington law. One such example is that of Nancy. Hers was not an easy life. She worked long hours as a waitress. She divorced her hard drinking first husband. The final judgment gave her the homestead, some cash and securities, and sole custody of their son. After the divorce Nancy had her attorney prepare a Will leaving all she owned to her son, Richard.

Some years later she met and married Harry, a chef at the restaurant where she worked. He moved into her home and they later had twin girls. Richard was 19, and his stepsisters 12, when Nancy died after a lengthy battle with cancer.

Nancy did not leave much — cash and securities worth $70,000, a car, and the homestead, all of which were in her name only.

Before she died, she told Richard, that she had not changed her Will because she wanted him to have all she owned. She said Harry had a good job and she was sure he would take good care of their daughters.

No sooner was the funeral over, when Nancy's son came in and demanded that Harry vacate his mother's home. Harry was furious and went to his attorney.

"I was a good husband to Nancy, supporting and taking care of her all during her illness. It was me, and not her son, who was at her side when she died. Don't I have any rights? And what about the twins. Don't they have any rights?"

The attorney explained "Nancy made the Will before she met and married you. Because she did not change her Will, you are considered to be an *omitted spouse*. Under Washington law you are entitled to receive as much as if she died without a Will. The same holds for the twins. They were born after the Will was made, so each of them is entitled to inherit what they would have inherited had Nancy died without a Will."

Harry said "O.K. I'll settle for that."

"Not so fast. The Court will need to have a hearing on the matter. If Richard can prove to the Court that Nancy intentionally wanted you and the twins to be omitted from the Will, then it may happen that you and the twins receive nothing."

Harry wondered "Don't I have Dower rights or something?"

"Dower rights are for widows. Curtesy rights are for widowers. In Washington those rights were abolished long before you were married. But you are entitled to ask the Court to award a Family Allowance to you and the twins" (RCW 11.04.060, 11.54.010).

Harry raised his objection to the Will to the Court. The court battle waged was lengthy, bitter and expensive. After hearing all of the evidence the Court found that Nancy intentionally did not provide for Harry and the twins. The Court also ruled that Harry and the twins were to receive a substantial Family Allowance.

There wasn't much left after the Family Allowance, medical bills, funeral expenses, attorney's fees and expenses of Probate administration were paid.

No doubt Nancy did not understand what would happen to her Estate once she passed on. The Will she left did not accomplish her goal of providing for her son. Had she consulted with an attorney she could have set up an Estate Plan that could have provided for Richard and avoided the costly court battle. More importantly, it may have saved Richard from becoming estranged from his stepfather and sisters at a time in his life when he was sorely in need of familial support.

But, the moral of the story, for the purpose of this discussion, is that if you believe that the decedent's Will is not valid or is not drafted according to Washington law, then you need to consult with an attorney experienced in Probate matters to determine your legal rights under the Will.

Getting Possession Of The Property

Knowing who is entitled to receive the decedent's property is one thing. Getting that property is another. As explained in the previous chapter if the decedent held property jointly with someone, or in a trust for someone, the property now belongs to the joint owner or beneficiary. If it is personal property such as a bank account or a security, the beneficiary can usually get possession of the property by giving a certified copy of the death certificate to the financial institution.

If the decedent had real or personal property in his name only, or if he held property as a Tenant In Common, then some sort of Probate procedure may be necessary in order to transfer ownership to the proper beneficiary. The assistance of an attorney may be required should a full Probate procedure be necessary, but there are many items that can be transferred without legal assistance. This chapter explains how to get possession of those items.

The chapter also contains an explanation of the different kinds of Probate procedures and when it is appropriate to use that procedure.

DISTRIBUTING PERSONAL PROPERTY

Too often, the first person to discover the body will help himself to the decedent's **personal effects** (clothing, jewelry, appliances, electrical equipment, cameras, books, stamp or coin collection, household items and furnishing, etc.). Unless that person is the decedent's sole beneficiary, such action is unconscionable, if not illegal.

If the decedent was married, then all of their Community Property now belongs to the surviving spouse. His Separate Property will be distributed according to his Will or their Community Property Agreement. If there is no Will or Community Property Agreement, then the decedent's personal property is distributed according to Washington's Laws of Descent.

The decedent may have left a separate writing leaving certain items of personal property to named beneficiaries. To be distributed as part of a Probate procedure, the decedent's Will needs to refer to the list, and the list must be in the decedent's own hand or if typed, the decedent's signature needs to appear at the end of the list (RCW 11.12.260). If no Probate procedure is necessary, the item can just be given to the named beneficiary.

If the decedent was not married, his personal effects should be given to the person appointed as the Personal Representative. The Representative has the duty to distribute the property according to the decedent's Will, or according to the Washington Laws of Descent, if he died without a Will.

If you determine that there is no need for a Probate procedure and the decedent did not have a Will then his next of kin need to divide all of the personal effects among themselves in approximately equal proportions.

What's Equal?

The decedent's Will or if no Will, then Washington's Laws of Descent and Distribution may direct that the decedent's personal property be divided equally between two or more beneficiaries. The problem with the term "equal" is that people have different ideas of what "equal" means. Unless there is clear evidence that the decedent's Will meant something else, "equal" refers to the monetary value of the item and not to the number of items received. For example, to divide the decedent's personal effects equally, one beneficiary may receive an expensive item of jewelry and another beneficiary may receive several items whose overall value is approximately equal to that single piece of jewelry.

When distributing personal effects there needs to be cooperation and perhaps compromise, or else bitter arguments might arise over items of little monetary value. One such argument occurred when an elderly woman died who was rich only in her love for her five children and nine grandchildren. After the funeral, the children gathered in their mother's apartment. Each child had his/her own furnishings and no need for anything in the apartment. They agreed to donate all of their mother's personal effects to a local charity with the exception of a few items of sentimental value.

Each child took some small item as a remembrance — a handkerchief, a large platter that their mother used to serve family dinners, a doily their mother crocheted. Things went smoothly until it came to her photograph album. Frank, the youngest sibling, said, "I'll take this." Marie objected saying "But there are pictures in that album that I want."

Frank retorted, "You already took all the pictures Mom had on her dresser."

The argument went downhill from there. Unsettled sibling rivalries boiled over, fueled by the hurt of the loss that they were all experiencing.

It almost came to blows when the eldest settled the argument: "Frank you make copies of all of the photos in the album for Marie. Marie, you make copies of all of the pictures that you took and give them to Frank. This way you both will have a complete set of Mom's pictures. And while you're at it, make copies for the rest of us."

NONPROBATE TRANSFERS

A *Nonprobate Asset* is something owned by the decedent that can be transferred to his beneficiary without the need for Probate. This includes real property held as joint tenants, as well as bank accounts held in trust for a beneficiary, and property covered by a Community Property Agreement.

Even though you take possession of the Nonprobate Asset, you need to keep in mind that if the decedent could have used that property to pay his bills during his lifetime, then that property is still available to pay his debts. In fact, if there is a Probate procedure, the bank or financial institution holding the Nonprobate Asset may require permission from the Personal Representative before they agree to turn over the property to you. Unless the decedent made some other provision for the payment of monies needed to settle the Estate, the Personal Representative has the right to ask you to contribute as much money from your inheritance as may be needed to pay your share of the decedents debts, taxes, and the cost of the Probate administration (RCW 11.04.250, 11.11.090, 11.18.200).

TRANSFERRING THE CAR

If the decedent owned a motor vehicle in his name only, then title to the car needs to be transferred to the new owner. The new owner needs to register the car in the state where it will be driven. You may want to limit the use of the car until it is transferred to the beneficiary. If the decedent's car is involved in an accident before the car is transferred to the new owner, then the decedent's Estate may be liable for the damage. Having adequate insurance on the car may save the Estate from monetary loss, but a pending lawsuit could delay Probate and prevent any money from being distributed to the beneficiaries until the lawsuit is settled.

If the decedent's car was included as part of a recorded Community Property Agreement, then the car belongs to the surviving spouse. The spouse can go to the local County Auditor or Sub-Agent Licensing Office and make the transfer. If there is no Community Property Agreement, the surviving spouse may want to ask the Court to include the car as part of the Family Allowance (see Page 97).

If there is a Probate procedure then it is the Personal Representative's job to transfer the motor vehicles to the proper beneficiary. If the decedent had a Will and he made a specific gift of the car to someone, then the Personal Representative will transfer the car to that person. If there was no mention of the car in his Will, and the car is not included as part of the Family Allowance, then the car goes to the *residuary beneficiaries* under the Will, i.e., those who inherit whatever is left once all the bills have been paid and all the special gifts made in the Will are distributed. If the decedent did not have a Will, then the car goes to the decedent's heirs as determined by Washington's Laws of Descent.

TRANSFER WHEN MORE THAN ONE BENEFICIARY

If there is more than one person who has the right to inherit the car, then they all can take title to the car. That may not be a practical thing to do since only one person can drive the car at any given time and if one gets into an accident, then they all can be held liable. The better route is for the beneficiaries to agree to have one person take title to the car. The person taking title will need to compensate the others for their share of the car. In such case the beneficiaries need to come to an agreement as to the value of the car.

DETERMINING THE VALUE OF THE CAR

Cars are valued in different ways. The *collateral* value of the car is the value that banks use to evaluate the car for purposes of making a loan to the owner of the car. If you were to trade in a car for the purpose of purchasing a new car, the car dealer would offer you the *wholesale* value of the car. Were you to purchase that same car from a car dealer, then he would price it at its *retail* or *fair market value*. Usually the retail price is highest, wholesale is lowest and the collateral value of the car is somewhere in between. You can determine these values via the Internet. The Web site for the Kelly Blue Book gives Low, Average and High Blue Book Values which corresponds to the wholesale, collateral and retail values.

Once the fair market value of the car is determined, the beneficiary who takes the car will be considered to have received that value as part of his inheritance. If none of the beneficiaries want the car, the Personal Representative will sell it and add the proceeds to the amount distributed to the beneficiaries.

MAKING THE TRANSFER

As explained, the surviving spouse can have title to the motor vehicle transferred by taking a certified copy of the death certificate and the Community Property Agreement to the local County Auditor or Sub-Agent Licensing Office. If there is no Community Property Agreement and no Probate necessary, the surviving spouse (or whoever is beneficiary) can get the car by signing an Affidavit of Inheritance (see page 149). It is a good idea to first call the Department of Licensing to determine the cost of the transfer and what information they will require of you. You can look them up in the telephone book under LICENSE SERVICES, or you can find the location of the office nearest you via the Internet.

 WASHINGTON STATE DEPARTMENT OF LICENSING
http://www.wa.gov/dol

TRANSFERRING WATERCRAFT AND SNOWMOBILES

In Washington, any motored watercraft or a sailboat that is 16′ or more in length is required to be titled and registered. If the decedent owned such a watercraft, then the title and registration certificate need to be transferred in the same manner as a motor vehicle. If the decedent owned a snowmobile, then its title and registration need to transferred as well.

REPORTING THE SALE
If you sell or transfer the decedent's motor vehicle or vessel, you must, within 5 days of the transfer, file a REPORT OF SALE with the Department of Licensing. You can download the form for the Report of Sale from the above Department of Licensing Web site (RCW 46.10.040, 46.12.101, 46.55).

CANCELING THE DRIVER'S LICENSE

It is important to notify the Department of Licensing of the death and to turn in the decedent's driver's license or photo identification card record. You can do this by writing "Deceased" across the driver's licence and mailing it to: THE DEPARTMENT OF LICENSING
P.O. Box 9909
Olympia, WA 98507-8500

The Department will take the decedent off their mailing list. This will assist the Department in preventing others from using the decedent's name for fraudulent purposes.

TRANSFERRING THE MOBILE HOME

Before transferring the decedent's mobile home, you need to determine whether he owned or leased the land under the mobile home. If he was renting space in a trailer park, you need to contact the trailer park owner to transfer the lease agreement to the beneficiary of the mobile home. If the decedent owned the land under the mobile home, then a Probate procedure will be necessary to transfer that land to the proper beneficiary. See page 153 for information about transferring real property.

The transfer of the mobile home itself is made much the same as any other motor vehicle, however, before allowing the transfer the Department of Licensing of the County Auditor will notify the County Assessor in the county where the mobile home is located of the change of ownership. Before they will allow the transfer they will require proof that all property taxes have been paid. The County Treasurer will need to prepare a certificate saying that all property taxes have been paid. If the mobile home is being sold, the County Treasurer will need to stamp a copy of the Real Estate Excise Tax Affidavit showing that taxes on the sale of the property have been paid (RCW 46.12.105).

The leased car is not an asset of the Estate because the decedent did not own the car. The leased car is a liability to the Estate because the decedent was obligated to pay the balance of the monies owed on the lease agreement. The Personal Representative, or next of kin, needs to work out an agreement with the company to either assign the lease to a beneficiary or family member who will agree to pay for the lease or to have the Estate pay off the lease by purchasing the car under the terms of the lease agreement.

Some lenders will allow the lease to be assigned to a beneficiary provided the Estate remains liable for the balance of payment. In such cases, it is better to have the beneficiary refinance the car and have the original lease agreement paid in full.

If the remaining payments exceed the current market value of the car, there may be a temptation to hand the keys over to the leasing company. This may not be the best strategy, because the leasing company can then sell the car and then sue the Estate for the balance of the monies owed. If the decedent had no assets or if the only assets he had are creditor proof, then simply returning the car may be an option. But if the decedent's Estate has assets available to pay the balance of the lease payments, then the Personal Representative needs to arrange to have the car transferred in a way that releases the Estate from all further liability.

INCOME TAX REFUND

Any refund due to the decedent under a joint federal income tax return filed by his surviving spouse will be sent to the surviving spouse. If the decedent's Personal Representative filed the final return, then the refund check will be sent to him to be deposited to the Estate account.

If the decedent was single and no Probate procedure is necessary, then whoever is entitled to decedent's Estate is entitled to the refund check. If you are the beneficiary of the decedent's Estate, you can obtain the refund by filing IRS form 1310 along with the decedent's final income tax return (the 1040). You can obtain form 1310 from the decedent's accountant, or if he did not have an accountant and you wish to file yourself, you can call the IRS at (800) 829-3676 to obtain the form.

You can download instructions, publications and forms from the Internal Revenue Service by going to the FORMS AND PUBLICATIONS section of the their Web site.

 INTERNAL REVENUE SERVICE
http://www.irs.gov/

The Personal Representative does not need to file form 1310 because once he files the decedent's final income tax return, any refund will be forwarded to him. Similarly, it is not necessary for the surviving spouse who filed a joint return to file form 1310.

SPOUSE	CREDIT UNION TRANSFER TO SPOUSE UP TO $1,000

Up to $1,000 on deposit in a Credit Union account held in the decedent's name only may be transferred to the surviving spouse without any need for a Probate procedure. If it later happens that a Personal Representative is appointed, the surviving spouse is required to account to the Personal Representative for the monies that were withdrawn. To get the money in the Credit Union, all the surviving spouse need do is to give them an Affidavit as follows:

AFFIDAVIT PURSUANT TO WASHINGTON STATUTE 11.62.030
Affiant declares that the following is true:
1. Affiant is the surviving spouse of _____
(name) who was a member of the _____
Credit Union. A certified copy of the death certificate is attached hereto.
2. No executor or administrator has been appointed for the member's Estate.
3. The deceased member had on deposit in said credit union money not exceeding the sum of $1,000.

This Affidavit is given for the purpose of receiving the balance of said account.

_____
Affiant Signature

State of _____
County of _____

Signed and sworn (or affirmed) before me on _____date by _____(name of Affiant).

_____
Notary Signature and Seal

TRANSFER OF SECURITIES TO SURVIVING SPOUSE

Any and all securities held in the decedent's name only (or jointly with the surviving spouse) may be transferred to the surviving spouse without any need for a Probate procedure, provided there is a Community Property Agreement. To get the securities transferred, the surviving spouse will need to give the transfer agent an Affidavit in the following form:

AFFIDAVIT PURSUANT TO WASHINGTON STATUTE 11.02.120
Affiant declares that the following is true:
1. Affiant is the surviving spouse of _____ (name). A certified copy of the death certificate is attached hereto.
2. At the time of his death the decedent owned the following described shares and/or securities _____
These shares or securities constituted community property of the spouses at the date of death of the deceased spouse and their disposition is controlled by the community property agreement. A copy of the community property agreement, certified by the auditor in the county where the agreement is recorded, is attached hereto.
3. No proceedings have been instituted to contest or set aside or cancel the agreement.
4. The claims of creditors have been paid or provided for.

This Affidavit is given for the purpose of transferring the above described securities to the surviving spouse.

_____
Affiant Signature

State of _____
County of _____
Signed and sworn (or affirmed) before me on _____date
by _____(name of Affiant).

_____
Notary Signature and Seal

FINAL WAGES

An Affidavit can be used to transfer the decedent's final wages to his spouse, provided no one has been appointed as Personal Representative, and the wages are not greater than $2,500. If the employer is the state of Washington, then that amount is increased to $10,000**. If the decedent's final wages exceed the given amount, and there is a Community Property Agreement giving all of his wages to his surviving spouse, the employer can transfer the wages to the surviving spouse. All the spouse need do is give the employer a copy of their Community Property Agreement and an Affidavit saying that the parties entered into the Agreement in good faith, and it was not rescinded (cancelled) prior to his death (RCW 49.48.120).

If there is no surviving spouse, the employer can transfer the funds to the following family members:
- ➪ the decedent's child or children
- ➪ the father or mother

Again, the employer will want an Affidavit saying that no Personal Representative was appointed, and the family member is entitled to the property. If the wages are greater than $2,500 (or $10,000 for an employee of Washington state) and do not exceed $60,000, whoever is entitled to the property can get the wages by using an AFFIDAVIT OF INHERITANCE as described on the next page.

**This is the 2003 value. The Washington State Director of Financial Management may make cost of living adjustments every two years.

THE SMALL ESTATE AFFIDAVIT

As discussed, the surviving spouse can use an Affidavit to transfer Community Property. An Affidavit can also be used to transfer Separate personal property, and even personal property inherited by the beneficiary of a single person. The beneficiary of the property can have the personal property transferred without a Probate procedure provided all of the following are true:

⇨ The decedent's entire Probate Estate, not counting Community property that may be subject to Probate, and not counting monies owed on the property, does not exceed $60,000.

⇨ 40 days have passed since the decedent's death.

⇨ No one has applied to be appointed as Personal Representative.

⇨ All debts, including the decedent's funeral and burial expenses have been paid; or arrangements have been made to pay them.

⇨ The person who is claiming the property is entitled to it according to RCW 11.62.005, because he is a beneficiary under the decedent's last valid Will or if no Will, according to the Laws of Descent - or - if a surviving spouse, entitled to the property as part of his/her share of their Community Property.

⇨ Written notice was sent to all other successors, and at least 10 days have passed since the notice was sent.

⇨ A copy of the Affidavit, and the decedent's Social Security number has been mailed to the State of Washington, Department of Social and Health Services, Office of Financial Recovery. Their address is: State of Washington, Dept. of Social and Health Services
Office of Financial Recovery
712 Pear Street S.E.
Olympia, WA   98507

A sample Affidavit appears on the next page.

AFFIDAVIT OF INHERITANCE
Pursuant to RCW 11.62.010

Affiant declares that the following is true:

1. Affiant, whose name and address are

_____

is entitled to the property as a successor as defined by RCW 11.62.005.

2. The decedent _____(name) whose Social Security number is _____ was a resident of the State of Washington.

3. At least 40 days have passed from his date of death. A certified copy of the death certificate is attached hereto.

4. The value of the decedent's entire Estate subject to probate (not including the surviving spouse's community property interest in any assets which are subject to probate in the decedent's Estate) wherever located, less liens and encumbrances, does not exceed $60,000.

5. No application or petition for the appointment of a personal representative is pending or has been granted in any jurisdiction.

6. All the debts of the decedent including funeral and burial expenses have been paid or provided for.

7. A description of the personal property and the portion thereof claimed is attached hereto. This personal property is subject to probate.

7. Affiant has given written notice either by personal service or by mail, identifying Affiant's claim, and describing the property that Affiant is claiming, to all other successors of the decedent. At least 10 days have elapsed since the service or mailing of such notice.

8. Affiant, as the claiming successor, is either personally entitled to full payment or delivery of the property claimed or is entitled to full payment or delivery thereof on the behalf and with the written authority of all other successors who have an interest therein.

9. A copy of this Affidavit, including the decedent's Social Security number, shall be mailed to the state of Washington, Department of Social and Health Services, Office of Financial Recovery.

_____
                    Affiant Signature

State of Washington
County of _____

Sign and sworn (or affirmed) before me on _____ date
by _____(name of Affiant).

_____
              Notary Signature and Seal

IS THIS TOO GOOD TO BE TRUE?

This seems almost too easy. The reader may be thinking "You mean that all I need to do is go to a brokerage office, or bank, give them an Affidavit and they will hand over the decedent's personal property?"

The answer is "yes, but..."

▶ YOU NEED PERMISSION FROM OTHER HEIRS ◀

If the decedent died leaving everything to one or two beneficiaries, and property of $60,000 or less and no real property involved, then the Affidavit is a simple way to go. If there are two heirs then they can sign a joint Affidavit to get the property. If several people are entitled to receive some part of the Estate, then you need to give each and every one of them written notice and get their permission to take possession of the property (See items 7 and 8 of the Affidavit). If one of the heirs refuses to give you permission, or if you are unable to contact an heir, or if you are not 100% sure of the identity of each and every heir, then you cannot use the Affidavit, and a Probate procedure will be necessary.

▶ THE TRANSFER CAN BE REFUSED ◀

The person in possession of the decedent's property needs to be reasonably certain of your identity and your right to the possession of the property. The person or financial institution in possession of the property might refuse to make the transfer if they get Affidavits from more than one person, or if they are concerned that there is fraud or misrepresentation. In such case, they have the right to turn over the asset to the Court and ask the Court to decide who should receive the property (RCW 11.62.020).

Before using the Affidavit, you need to either pay all of the decedent's debts or see to it that arrangements have been made for their payment. But it could happen that the decedent owed money that you know nothing about. Any creditor has two years to come forward and demand payment from whomever has possession of the decedent's property (that's you). As explained on page 88, you can shorten that period to 4 months by publishing notice in a legal newspaper as a Notice Agent (RCW 11.10.040, 11.42.050).

If you suspect that there may not be sufficient funds in the Probate Estate to pay all debts, it is better to have a full Probate procedure and let the Court decide how much each creditor is paid. Once appointed, the Personal Representative can require that anyone who inherited a Nonprobate Asset to contribute their share of monies owed. If you just take possession of the property without going through Probate you will not have any authority to require contributions from the beneficiary of the Nonprobate asset.

Better to let the Personal Representative settle the Estate if there is any chance that there may be a creditor problem. The Personal Representative can follow the directions of the Court without any personal liability to himself or to the beneficiaries of the Estate. All of the beneficiaries can walk away from the situation without the fear of being personally hounded to pay for the decedent's debts.

TRANSFERRING REAL PROPERTY

As explained in Chapter 5, no Probate procedure is necessary to transfer real property if the decedent held that property:

⇨ as Joint Tenants - or -

⇨ as the owner of a Life Estate - or -

⇨ as part of a Community Property Agreement that is recorded in the county where the property is located.

The surviving joint party owns the property as of the date of death, however, the decedent's name remains on the deed. Anyone examining title to the property will not know of the death. The Washington Vital Records Department is responsible to issue the death certificate, but not to publish it as part of the public record. Of course, if there happens to be a Probate procedure, anyone can look up those public records and learn of the death.

If no Probate procedure is necessary, then the surviving owner (or the remainder beneficiary of the Life Estate) needs to keep a certified copy of the death certificate available in the event they want to sell or transfer the property at a later date.

If the decedent held real property in his name only or jointly with another as Tenants In Common, then a Probate procedure is necessary. The attorney for the Personal Representative will arrange to have the decedent's real property transferred to the proper beneficiary, and that transfer will be recorded as part of the public record. If you are the new owner, you should receive all of the original recorded documents to keep for your records.

TRANSFERRING OUT OF STATE PROPERTY HELD JOINTLY

Each state regulates the transfer of real property within that state. Many states have rules much like Washington, i.e., no document need be recorded to transfer real property to a joint tenant who has a right of survivorship, or to a remainder beneficiary of a Life Estate interest. It is the practice in some states, such as Ohio and Illinois, to record an Affidavit that describes the transfer of the property to the surviving owner. Some states, such as Florida, allow the death certificate to be recorded in the count where the property is located, so that anyone examining title to the property will know who now owns the property.

If the decedent owned out of state real property jointly with rights of survivorship, or if he held a Life Estate interest, you may want to call the recording department in the county where the property is located to find out what documents (if any) need to recorded to let people know that the surviving joint tenant (or remainder beneficiary) now owns the property. The name of the official in charge of recording deeds varies state to state. Here in Washington, the County Auditor serves as the recorder of deeds (RCW 36.22.010). In other states it could be the County Registrar or the County Recorder, or the Clerk of the Circuit Court.

Of course, if the decedent owned real property in his own name or as a Tenant In Common, you need to contact an attorney in that state to have the property transferred to the proper beneficiary.

THE FULL PROBATE PROCEDURE

There needs to be a full Probate procedure if the decedent left real property in his name only or as a Tenant In Common; or if he left personal property worth more than $60,000. The procedure can take anywhere from several months to more than a year depending on the size and complexity of the Probate Estate. A Personal Representative must be appointed and Letters issued.

APPOINTING THE PERSONAL REPRESENTATIVE

Washington statute gives an order of priority in the appointment of Personal Representative. Whoever the decedent named as Executor in his Will has top priority. If there is Community Property, then the surviving spouse has the right to administer that property regardless of whom the decedent named as Executor of the Will. This means, that the surviving spouse has the right to be the Personal Representative of the decedent's half of their Community Property, provided the surviving spouse asks to do so within 40 days from the date of death. If the surviving spouse administers the Community Property, the person named as Executor may only administer the decedent's Separate Property (RCW 11.28.030).

If the decedent died without a Will, then the surviving spouse has the right to be Personal Representative, or to name someone to serve. If there is no surviving spouse, the following people have priority in the given order:
⇨   child, parent, sibling, grandchild, niece/nephew
⇨   any fiduciary (Trustee, Guardian, Attorney-In-Fact) who controlled substantially all of the decedent's assets
⇨   the Director of Revenue
⇨   a principal creditor
⇨   someone chosen by the Court (RCW 11.28.120).

NONINTERVENTION VS. SUPERVISED ADMINISTRATION

A full Probate administration can be an involved, time consuming, and expensive, procedure. Many steps in the procedure involve going before the Court to get permission to take certain action, such as paying a disputed bill, or distributing property to a beneficiary. If there is one beneficiary, and no problem paying monies owed, then it is a waste of the Court's time and the Estate's money to go through unnecessary formalities. Washington statute allows a Personal Representative to petition (ask) the Court for *Nonintervention Powers* i.e., power to settle the Estate without Court supervision (RCW 11.68.011).

The Court will grant the request if there is enough money to pay all the bills and the Personal Representative is the named Executor of the Will, and the Will does not require a supervised administration. If the decedent died without a Will, and the surviving spouse is the Personal Representative, then the Court will grant Nonintervention powers, provided the Probate Estate consists of Community Property only, and there are no children of the decedent who are not also children of the surviving spouse. In all other cases, the Court will hold a hearing on the matter. Any interested party can appear at the hearing and raise any objection they may have. No hearing is necessary if all interested parties *waive* (give up) their right to object (RCW 11.68.041, 11.68.050).

It is easier for the Representative to administer the Estate with Nonintervention Powers. He can pay bills, mortgage, lease, sell and transfer Estate property all without court supervision (RCW 11.68.090). But the downside is that the Personal Representative can do some serious mischief if he is not trustworthy. Although, it may cost more to administer an Estate with Court supervision, in the long run it may worth it.

YOUR RIGHTS AS A BENEFICIARY

The Personal Representative is in charge of settling the Estate. Too often, beneficiaries of the Estate have no idea of what is going on. They wait to receive their inheritance, not knowing that they rights under Washington law; and more importantly, not knowing how to assert their rights.

✧ RIGHT TO A COPY OF THE WILL

If there is a Will, then you have the right to receive a copy of that Will. Once the Personal Representative is appointed have him or his attorney forward the copy to you.

✧ RIGHT TO YOUR OWN ATTORNEY

The attorney who handles the Estate is employed by, and represents, the Personal Representative. If the Estate is sizeable, then you might consider employing your own attorney to check that things are done properly and in a timely manner. Even if the Estate is small, or if the Probate procedure is unsupervised, consider consulting with an attorney if at any time you are concerned about the way the Probate is being conducted.

✧ RIGHT TO OBJECT TO PERSONAL REPRESENTATIVE

Within 20 days of his appointment, the Personal Representative is required to give written notice to each and every beneficiary of the Estate that he has been appointed (RCW 11.28.237). It may be that he has been granted Nonintervention Powers from the Court, without any hearing on the matter. As soon as you learn of his appointment, you should ask him whether he has received or will seek such powers. If you have any concern about who has been appointed to serve as Personal Representative or about the granting of Nonintervention Powers, then this is the time to bring those concerns to the attention of the Court.

✧ RIGHT TO APPEAR BEFORE THE COURT

You have the right to go before the Court on your own, but before doing so, you should consult with an experienced Probate attorney. He can explain the best way for you to present your concerns to the Court. He can tell you what arguments have a good chance of swaying the Judge. And he can tell you which arguments have so little probability of success that they are not worth pursuing.

✧ RIGHT TO DEMAND SUFFICIENT BOND

It doesn't happen often, but every now and again a Personal Representative will run off with Estate funds. A bond is insurance for the Estate. If Estate monies are stolen then the company that issued the bond will reimburse the Estate for the loss. It is up to the Court to decide whether a bond is necessary, and if so, the value of the bond. The Court will not require a bond if the Personal Representative is an authorized bank or trust company or the surviving spouse. And, in most cases, the Court will not require a bond if the Will asks that no bond be given (RCW 11.28.185).

Most Wills state that no bond shall be required. The reason is two-fold. The Will maker chooses someone he trusts to administer the Estate, so he does not think a bond is necessary. And there are economic reasons. The cost of the bond is paid for by the Estate, and ultimately the amount inherited is reduced by the amount paid for the bond. Of course, the cost of the bond should not be a factor, if there is any danger of the Estate property belong lost or mismanaged. If you are concerned about the safety of the Estate assets, then you need to bring these concerns to the attention of the Court, and ask the Court to require the Personal Representative to be bonded.

✧ RIGHT TO BE KEPT INFORMED

If the Court is supervising the procedure, the Personal Representative may need to petition the Court for permission to sell property or to settle a disputed claim or to continue operating the decedent's business. Anytime after the Personal Representative is appointed, you can file a request with the Clerk of the Probate Court that you wish to receive a copy of every accounting and petition that is filed. You need to mail a copy of that request to the Personal Representative or his attorney (RCW 11.28.240).

A Personal Representative who has been granted Nonintervention Powers does not need to ask Court permission to do these things. All you as a beneficiary can do, is wait to receive your share of the inheritance. Of course you can unofficially contact the Personal Representative, and ask for information about how things are going. But if he refuses to give you that information, then unless he is downright dishonest or grossly negligent, there isn't much you can do until a year has passed. Once a year has passed, you have the right to ask the Court to order an accounting. That accounting can include:

📄 a description of all of the property that has come into the hands of the Personal Representative;

📄 a statement of all payments and distributions;

📄 a statement of all of the claims that have been filed against the Estate;

📄 a copy of all tax returns filed by the Representative (RCW 11.68.065).

Even though the Court can force an accounting, the Court cannot require a Personal Representative with Nonintervention Powers to close the Estate. In some cases the Probate procedure has continued for well over seven years (*Estate of Ardell*, 96 Wn. App. 708, 980 P.2d 771(1999)).

✧ RIGHT TO COPY OF INVENTORY

The Personal Representative must prepare an inventory of all of the assets of the Probate Estate within three months of his appointment. He is not required to send a copy of the inventory to anyone, but if an interested party asks for a copy, then he must mail it out within 10 days of the request. The interested party could be a beneficiary of the Probate Estate, or creditor who filed a claim, or the Department of Revenue, or even the beneficiary of a Nonprobate asset who was asked to contribute to the cost of the Probate administration. The Personal Representative is not required to employ an appraiser to assist with the evaluation; so if you are not satisfied with the value assigned to any item, you may want to request an independent appraisal of that item (RCW 11.44.015).

✧ RIGHT TO KNOW PERSONAL REPRESENTATIVE'S FEE

The Personal Representative has a right to be compensated for his efforts in settling the Estate. If the Personal Representative is also a beneficiary of the Estate he may decide not to take a fee and just take his inheritance. The reason may be economic. Any fee the Personal Representative takes is taxable as ordinary income, but monies inherited are not taxable to him as a beneficiary. Ask the Personal Representative to tell you, in writing, whether he intends to ask for a fee, and if so, how much. If you believe that fee to be excessive, you can raise those concerns to the Court. Unless the fee is stated in the Will, the Court will determine what is a just and reasonable fee for the Personal Representative (RCW 11.48.210).

✧ RIGHT TO KNOW THE ATTORNEY'S FEES

It is the Personal Representative's job to use the Probate Estate to pay all valid claims and then to distribute what is left to the proper beneficiary. Debts are paid from the decedent's Estate and not from the Representative's pocket; but if the Personal Representative makes a mistake, he may be responsible to pay for it. For example, the Personal Representative may be liable if he distributes the Estate to the beneficiaries without paying sufficient state taxes. In such case the taxes will come out of his own pocket, unless he can convince the beneficiaries to contribute whatever is needed (RCW 83.100.120).

The Personal Representative has the right to employ an attorney to guide him through the procedure so that things will be done properly and at no personal cost to the Representative. It is proper to have the attorney paid with Estate funds (RCW 11.48.210). You, as a beneficiary, have the right to know how much will be charged for legal fees. Ask the Personal Representative to give you a copy of the retainer agreement. Some firms charge a single flat fee for the procedure. Others charge on an hourly basis.

If you think the fee is excessive, you could call different law firms and ask what they charge to Probate an Estate with similar assets, and that will give you some idea of the going rate. If after doing some "comparison shopping" you believe that the proposed fees are unreasonable, you can negotiate with them to lower the fee. If you are unsuccessful, then you can bring the matter before the Court. Before the Estate is finally closed, you have the right to have the Court determine whether fees paid to the Personal Representative, lawyers, accountants, and appraisers are reasonable.

✧ RIGHT TO FINAL ACCOUNTING

You as a beneficiary have the right to a final accounting. If the Estate is supervised, the Personal Representative must file a Final Report with the Court that contains an accounting of how Estate funds were spent, and how the Representative intends to distribute whatever funds are left (RCW 11.68.100, 11.76.030). You will receive a copy of the Final Report, unless you sign a waiver giving up your right to an accounting. If you are asked to sign a waiver, keep in mind that the accounting is for your benefit. There are few situations that justify you giving up your right to know how Estate monies were spent. If you have any question about the Final Report, then those questions must be answered to your satisfaction, before you agree to the proposed distribution. If the Estate has significant assets, you may want your own accountant to look over the accounting.

UNSUPERVISED ADMINISTRATION

A Personal Representative who has been granted Nonintervention Powers can close the Estate in one of two ways. He can do an accounting much like the Final Report filed in a supervised administration, or he can file a ***Declaration of Completion***. The Declaration simply says that the Estate is ready to be closed. It does not give an accounting, but it does state how much the Personal Representative, his attorney, the accountant and appraisers have been (or will be) paid. The Personal Representative must send a copy of the Declaration to you. You have the right to petition the Court for a final accounting and/or a review of these fees. If you do not make your request to the Court within 30 days of the day that the Declaration was filed, the fees and acts of the Personal Representative will be approved and Estate will be closed (RCW 11.68.110).

✧ RIGHT TO RECEIVE A DEBT FREE INHERITANCE

Once a beneficiary finally receives his inheritance, the last thing he wants to hear is that there is some unfinished business, or worse yet that monies need to be paid from the inheritance he received. But that is just what could happen if the Personal Representative distributes the money before all the creditors are paid. An unpaid creditor could sue the beneficiary any time within 24 months from the date of death if the Personal Representative neglected to pay a valid claim.

You can protect yourself from this unhappy situation by checking to see that the Personal Representative gave notice to all of the decedent's creditors, and then verifying that they were paid. This time period can be shortened to 30 days if the Personal Representative gives a known creditor written notice. If the Personal Representative publishes notice then creditors have 4 months from the first date of publication to come forward (RCW 11.42.050). The law does not require that the Personal Representative give any kind of notice, but you can tell the Representative that you want notice to be given (RCW 11.40.020). If he refuses, and he has not been granted Nonintervention powers, you can ask the Court to order him to do so.

Taxes are another concern. You should ask to see a copy of all of the tax returns that were filed, and then verify that any monies that were due have been paid. Most importantly, you should not agree to having the Estate closed if there are any outstanding debts that need to be paid. Once the Personal Representative is discharged by the Court, you lose your right to sue the Personal Representative for neglecting to do his job properly, or for some act of fraud or dishonesty he committed while performing of his duties (RCW 4.16.370, 11.96A.070).

✦ RIGHT TO HAVE EVERYONE CONTRIBUTE THEIR SHARE

Under Washington law, beneficiaries of the Probate assets and beneficiaries of Nonprobate assets are each responsible to contribute to their share of the decedent's debts, Estate taxes and cost of administration (RCW 11.18.200). For example suppose the decedent left a $50,000 Nonprobate asset, such as a joint bank account, and his homestead, a Probate asset worth $100,000.

The total value of the decedent's Estate is $150,000. Whoever receives the bank account must contribute his prorated share. In this case $50,000/$150,000 represents one-third of the Estate, so he must contribute one-third of all of the decedent's unpaid debts, funeral and burial expenses, Estate Taxes, and the costs of administration. You as the beneficiary of the Probate Estate have the right to demand that the Personal Representative see to it that the beneficiary of the account contributes his fair share.

IT'S YOUR RIGHT - DON'T BE INTIMIDATED

As a beneficiary, you have many legal rights, but you may feel uncomfortable asserting those rights with a friend or family member who is Personal Representative. Don't be. It's your money and your legal right to be kept informed. Be especially firm if the Personal Representative waves you off with:

"You've known me for years. Surely you trust me."

People who are trustworthy, don't ask to be trusted. They do what is right. The very fact that the Personal Representative is resisting is a red flag. In such situation, you can explain that it is not a matter of trust, but a matter of what is your legal right.

At the same time, keep things in perspective. Your relationship with the Personal Representative may be more important to you than the money you inherit. The job of settling an Estate can be complex and demanding. If the Personal Representative is getting the job done, then let him know that you appreciate his efforts.

THE CHECK LIST

We have discussed many things that need to be done when someone dies in the state of Washington. The next page contains a check list that you may find helpful.

You can check those items that you need to do, and then cross them off the list once they are done. We made the list as comprehensive as possible, so many items may not apply in your case. In such case, you can cross them off the list or mark them *N/A* (not applicable).

Things to do

FUNERAL ARRANGEMENTS TO BE MADE
- ☐ AUTOPSY ☐ ANATOMICAL GIFT
- ☐ DISPOSITION OF BODY OR ASHES

DEATH CERTIFICATE
- ☐ HAVE CERTIFICATE RECORDED

GIVE COPY TO: _____

_____

NOTICE OF DEATH
PEOPLE TO BE NOTIFIED _____

COMPANIES TO NOTIFY
- ☐ TELEPHONE COMPANY
  - ☐ LOCAL CARRIER ☐ LONG DISTANCE ☐ CELLULAR
- ☐ NEWSPAPER (OBITUARY PRINTED)
- ☐ NEWSPAPER CANCELLED   ☐ deposit refund
- ☐ SOCIAL SECURITY
- ☐ INTERNET SERVER
- ☐ TELEVISION CABLE COMPANY
- ☐ POWER & LIGHT   ☐ deposit refund
- ☐ POST OFFICE
- ☐ OTHER UTILITIES (GAS, WATER)   ☐ deposit refund
- ☐ PENSION PLAN
- ☐ ANNUITY
- ☐ HEALTH INSURANCE COMPANY
- ☐ LIFE INSURANCE COMPANY
- ☐ HOME INSURANCE COMPANY
- ☐ MOTOR VEHICLE INSURANCE COMPANY
- ☐ CONDOMINIUM OR HOMEOWNER ASSOCIATION
- ☐ CANCEL SERVICE CONTRACT   ☐ deposit refund
- ☐ CREDIT CARD COMPANIES _____

_____

_____

Things to do

REMOVE DECEDENT AS BENEFICIARY OF:
☐ WILL   ☐ INSURANCE POLICY   ☐ PENSION PLAN
☐ BANK OR IRA ACCOUNT   ☐ SECURITY

DEBTS
PAY DECEDENT'S DEBTS (AMOUNT & CREDITOR)

_____

COLLECT MONIES OWED TO DECEDENT (AMOUNT & DEBTOR)

_____

TAXES
☐ FILE FINAL FEDERAL INCOME TAX RETURN
☐ RECEIVE INCOME TAX REFUND
☐ FILE ESTATE TAX RETURN

PROPERTY TO BE TRANSFERRED
☐ PERSONAL EFFECTS
☐ MOTOR VEHICLE
☐ BANK ACCOUNT
☐ CREDIT UNION ACCOUNT
☐ IRA ACCOUNT
☐ SECURITIES
☐ BROKERAGE ACCOUNT
☐ INSURANCE PROCEEDS
☐ HOMESTEAD
☐ TIME SHARE
☐ OTHER REAL PROPERTY
☐ CONTENTS OF SAFE DEPOSIT BOX

OTHER THINGS TO DO

_____
_____
_____

Once the Probate procedure is over, you will be left with many documents and wonder which you need to keep:

COURT DOCUMENTS

You should keep a copy of the inventory to establish the value of property that you inherit. That value becomes your basis for any Capital Gains tax that you may need to pay in the future. Other than the inventory, there is no reason to keep any Court document, provided you are satisfied with the way things were done and do not intend to take action against the Personal Representative, or his attorney. The Clerk of the Superior Court keeps the Probate file on record. If for some reason you later need a copy of a Probate document, you can get it from the Clerk.

PERSONAL DOCUMENTS

You may wish to keep the decedent's personal papers (birth certificate, marriage certificate, naturalization papers, army records, religious documents, etc.) for your own personal records. You may want to keep the decedent's medical records in the event that member of the family needs to check out a genetic disease.

TAX RECORDS

The IRS has up to three years to collect additional taxes, and you have up to seven years to claim a loss from a worthless security, so you should keep the decedent's tax file for seven years from the date of filing the return. You can learn more about which records to keep from the IRS publication 552. You can get the publication by calling the IRS at (800) 829-3676 or you can download it from their Web site.

 IRS WEB SITE
http://www.irs.gov

Everyman's Estate Plan 7

The first six chapters of this book describe how to wind up the affairs of the decedent. As you read those chapters, you learned about the kinds of problems that can occur when settling the decedent's Estate. It is relatively simple for you to set up an Estate Plan so that your family members are not burdened with similar problems. An *Estate Plan* is the arranging of your finances for maximum control and protection during your lifetime, and at the same time ensuring that your property will be transferred quickly and at little cost to your heirs.

If you think that only wealthy people need to prepare an Estate Plan, you are mistaken. Each year, heirs of relatively modest estates, spend thousands of dollars to settle an Estate. A bit of planning could have eliminated most, if not all, of the expense and hassle suffered by those families.

The suggestions in this chapter are designed to assist the average person in preparing a practical and inexpensive Estate Plan, so we named this chapter EVERYMAN'S ESTATE PLAN.

Once you create your own Estate Plan, you can be assured that your family will not be left with more problems than happy memories of you.

AVOIDING PROBATE

TRUE OR FALSE?

(   ) If you have a Will, then there will need
        to be a Probate administration.

(   ) Probate is necessary if you don't have a Will.

(   ) Probate is necessary if you leave anything worth
        more than $25,000.

If you answered false to all of the above, you are either a lawyer, or you carefully read the chapters 5 and 6. All of these sentences are false because you may have arranged your property so that it passes to your beneficiaries automatically, without the need for Probate.

The point we were attempting to make is that:

> Whether a Probate procedure is necessary has nothing to do with whether there is a Will, or even how much money is involved. The determining factor is how the property is titled (owned).

There are three ways to title property:
- ✧ in your name only
- ✧ jointly with another
- ✧ in trust for another

It may be necessary to have a Probate procedure if you hold property in your name only. After reading Chapter 6, you may be thinking that Probate is a good thing to avoid. Holding property jointly with another or in trust for another has the benefit of avoiding Probate, but as with any Estate Plan, it is important to consider all the pros and cons.

OWNERSHIP OF BANK ACCOUNTS

You can arrange to have all of your bank accounts set up so that should you die the money goes directly to a beneficiary. For example, suppose all you own is a bank account and you want whatever you have in this account to go to your son and daughter when you die. You might think that a simple solution is to put each child's name on the account, but first consider the problems associated with a joint account:

⊠ POTENTIAL LIABILITY

If you hold a bank account jointly with your adult child and that child is sued or gets a divorce then the child may need to disclose his ownership of the joint account. In such a case, you may find yourself spending money to prove that the account was established for convenience only and that all of the money in that account really belongs to you.

⊠ OVERREACHING

If you set up a joint account with your child so that the child has authority to withdraw funds from the account, funds could be withdrawn without your knowledge or authorization. If you open a joint account with two of your children, then there is the problem of what happens to the funds after your death. According to Washington law each party to a joint account owns as much of the account as that party contributed to the account. Should one of the joint owners die, the law states that the share belonging to the decedent is to be divided equally between the surviving owners. But each if you open a joint account with both your children, each will have access to the account. After your death the first child to the bank may decide to withdraw all of the money and that will, at the very least, cause hard feelings between them (RCW 30.22.090, 30.22.100, 30.22.140)

THE BENEFICIARY ACCOUNT

Holding bank accounts jointly with your beneficiary eliminates the need for Probate, but at the cost of control of the funds during your lifetime. There are two ways to title your bank account so that it passes directly to your beneficiary, but without giving access to that property during your lifetime:

THE IN TRUST FOR ("ITF") ACCOUNT

You can direct a financial institution to hold your account *In Trust For* ("ITF") one or more beneficiaries that you name. Your contract with the bank will state that the beneficiary has no rights in the account until and unless you die.

THE PAY ON DEATH ("POD") ACCOUNT

You can have a contract with the bank that directs the bank to *Pay On Death* ("POD") all of the money in the account to one or more beneficiaries that you name.

With both the ITF and POD account:

⇨   During his lifetime the owner of the account is free to change beneficiaries without asking the beneficiary's permission to do so.

⇨   The beneficiary does not have access to the account until the owner of the account dies.

⇨   If there are two or more beneficiaries, then once the owner dies, the funds will be divided equally between the beneficiaries.

⇨   If there are two or more beneficiaries of the account, and one of them dies, the remaining beneficiaries will inherit the account, unless the owner of the account makes some other provision with the bank (RCW 30.22.090, 30.22.100).

TRANSFER ON DEATH SECURITIES

The Washington law for securities is much the same as the statutes for bank accounts. You can arrange to have a security (a stock, bond or brokerage account) transferred to a beneficiary upon your death. You can instruct the holder of the security to Pay On Death or TRANSFER ON DEATH ("TOD") to a named beneficiary. For example, a security can be titled as:

TIM REILLY and OLIVIA REILLY, JOINT TENANTS
TRANSFER ON DEATH TO STUART REILLY

The TOD designation (and the ITF or POD designation) have no effect on the community property rights of the parents. They remain the same with or without the TOD designation. The parents are free to change the beneficiary of the security at any time during their lifetime. Stuart has no right to the security until both his parents die. If no change is made, Stuart will inherit the security once both parents are deceased. If Stuart dies before his parents and no other provision made, then the security will go to the Estate of the last parent to die (RCW 21.35.030, 21.35.035).

If your Estate consists only of bank accounts and/or securities, and you want all of your property to go to one or two beneficiaries without the need for Probate, but with maximum control and protection of your funds during your lifetime, then holding your property in any of these beneficiary forms:

"In Trust For"
"Pay-On-Death"
"Transfer-On-Death"

should accomplish your goal.

GIFT TO A MINOR CHILD

At the beginning of this chapter, we identified two problems with a joint account: potential liability if the joint owner is sued and overreaching by the joint owner. If you wish to make a gift to a minor child, then that presents still another problem. The ITF, POD and TOD account avoids the problem of potential liability and overreaching, but if the beneficiary of such account is a minor, there is the problem of the a child having access to a large sum of money. A company in possession of the funds has the right to give amounts up to $30,000 to an adult member of the child's family. For amounts over $30,000, the law requires that the company get Court authorization to transfer the funds. The Court will probably require a guardianship be established to protect the funds until the child reaches 18 (RCW 11.114.070).

This presents a dilemma. If the amount given is no greater than $30,000, then the parent can spend the money for the minor as he/she sees fit. The child may never even know of your gift. You may think it best that the child inherits more than $30,000; this way a Court will see to it that the monies are held safely till the child reaches 18. But that only presents a new set of problems. It takes time, effort and money to set up a guardianship. If you leave the child a significant amount of money, then the Guardian has the right to charge to manage those funds. It could happen that the cost of the guardianship significantly reduces the amount of money inherited by the child.

There are ways to avoid the problem of having a Guardian appointed to care for property inherited by a child, and yet ensuring that the monies are protected. One way is to appoint a Custodian under the WASHINGTON UNIFORM TRANSFERS TO MINORS ACT.

THE UNIFORM TRANSFERS TO MINORS ACT

If you wish to leave property to a child, you can appoint someone to be the Custodian of the gift under the *Washington Uniform Transfers to Minors Act*. This law is designed to protect gifts made to a minor. It is appropriate to use this method if you want to give a child a gift of a security or a life insurance policy, or an interest in a real property or even tangible property such as an expensive painting. The gift can be made only to one child. If you wish to make a gift to two children, then you will need to make a separate gift to each of them (RCW 11.114.100).

To make a gift under the Washington Uniform Gifts to Minors Act, you need to name a trusted relative or friend or even a financial institution to be the Custodian of the gift. For example, suppose you have a bank account that you want given to your grandchild in the event of your death. You can have the bank hold the money in the account until the child reaches the age of 21 by naming the bank as custodian:

> POD FRIENDLY BANK as custodian for
> _____ (name of minor)
> under the Washington Transfers to Minors Act.

You can use the Washington Transfers to Minors Act as part of your Will. If you are making the gift as part of your Will then the law allows you to direct the Custodian to hold the money till the child is 21. If you die and the child is at least 21, then the Custodian will give the gift to the child. If the child is not yet 21, the Custodian will hold the gift for the benefit of the child (RCW 11.114.050, 11.114.090, 11.114.200).

The Custodian has the discretion to use the funds to care for the child. The Custodian can pay monies directly to the child, or can use the money for the child's benefit. The Custodian can refuse to use any of the monies for the child and just keep the funds invested until the child reaches 21.

If the Custodian wants to keep the funds invested, any interested person, such as a family member, or the child's Guardian, or even the child once he is 14, can ask the Probate Court to order the Custodian to part with some or all of the money. The Judge will decide what is in the child's best interest and then rule on the matter.

The Custodian needs to invest and manage the property in a responsible, prudent manner. He is entitled to be paid for his effort. If the gift is sizeable, then the Custodian's fee can be sizeable. Before appointing a person or a company as Custodian, it is best to come to a written agreement about what will be charged to manage the custodial property (RCW 11.114.120, 11.114.140, 11.114.150).

The Washington Transfers to Minors Act is good to use if you want a single gift to be given to a single person once he/she reaches the age of 21. If you want to provide for several children and have more flexibility about when they are to receive the gift, then a Trust may be the better way to go. We will discuss how to create a Trust later in this chapter.

THE GIFT OF REAL PROPERTY

As explained in Chapter 5, if you own real property together with another, then who owns the property upon your death depends on how the Grantee is identified on the face of the deed. If you compare the Grantee clause of the deed to the examples on pages 109 through 112 you can determine who will inherit the property should you die. If you are not satisfied with the way the property will be inherited, then you need to consult with an attorney to change the deed so that it will conform to your wishes.

If you own the property in your name only, then your beneficiaries will need to go through a Probate procedure. The only exception is if you are married, and you and your spouse have recorded a Community Property Agreement that transfers the real property to your surviving spouse (See page 113).

JOINT OWNERSHIP

If you hold property in your name only, and wish to avoid Probate, you can have your deed changed so that you and a beneficiary are joint owners with Right of Survivorship. If you do so then should either of you die, the other will own the property 100%. That avoids Probate but you will not be able to sell that property during your lifetime without the beneficiary's permission. And if the beneficiary gives permission and the property is sold, the beneficiary will have the legal right to half of the proceeds of the sale.

CAUTION   GIFT OF HOMESTEAD

Some elderly parents worry that they may need nursing care at some time in the future and lose all of their life savings to pay for that care. The parent may decide that the best way to avoid Probate and protect the homestead from loss is to transfer the homestead to their child with the understanding that the parent will continue to live there until he/she dies. But this is just trading risks.

☒ RISK OF LOSS

Property transferred to your child could be lost if the child runs into serious financial difficulties or gets sued. This is especially a risk if your child is a professional doctor, nurse, accountant, financial planner, attorney, etc.). If your child is (or gets) married, then this complicates matters even more so. If the child is divorced, the property will need to be included as part of the settlement agreement. This may be to your child's detriment because the child may need to share the value of the property with his/her former spouse. If you do not transfer the property, then it cannot become part of the marital equation.

☒ POSSIBLE LOSS OF GOVERNMENT BENEFITS

If you transfer property, then depending upon the value of the transfer, you could be disqualified from receiving Medicaid or Supplemental Security Income ("SSI") benefits for a substantial period of time. When a person applies for Medicaid, he must disclose if, within 3 years of his application, he transferred property for less than the full value (i.e. he gifted property). This reporting period extends to 5 years if the transfer was to a Trust. The Medicaid agency will compute a disqualification period depending on the value of the transfer. This can present a serious problem should you need extended nursing care during the disqualification period.

☒ LOSS OF HOMESTEAD CREDITOR PROTECTION

Washington law exempts up to $40,000 of the value of your homestead from the claims of your creditors (see Page 97). If you are sued and lose you cannot be forced to sell your homestead unless the equity in your property is greater than $40,000. Even if you are forced to sell, at least you get to keep up to $40,000 of the proceed. You lose this protection if you simply transfer your home to your child (RCW 6.13.030). If the child does not occupy that property as his homestead, then there is no homestead creditor protection whatsoever. The child's creditors can force the sale of the property (that's your home) for relatively small amounts of unpaid debts.

☒ LOSS OF HOMESTEAD TAX EXEMPTION

People over the age of 61, and those who are disabled are entitled to a Homestead Tax Exemption (see Page 37). If you are receiving this exemption and you gift the property to your child, you will lose this tax break. It could cost you more to continue to live in your own home.

☒ POSSIBLE CAPITAL GAINS TAX

If you gift the property to the child, when he sells the property he will be subject to a Capital Gains Tax on the increase in value from the price you paid to the selling price at the time of the sale. If you do not make the gift during your lifetime, the child will inherit the property with a step-up in basis, i.e., he will inherit the property at its market value as of the date of death. Under today's tax structure and continuing until 2009, that step-up in basis is unlimited. If your child sells the property when it is inherited, no Capital Gains Tax is due regardless of how large the step-up in basis. In 2010, there will be a limit on the amount that can be inherited free of the Capital Gains Tax; but that limit is quite high, so for most of us this is not a concern.

⊠ POSSIBLE GIFT TAX

If the value of the transfer is worth more than $11,000 you need to file a gift tax return. For most of us, this is not a problem because no gift tax need be paid unless the value of the property (plus the value of all gifts in excess of the Annual Gift Tax Exclusion that you gave over your lifetime) exceeds $1,000,000 (see Page 39). If your Estate is in that tax bracket, then you need to be aware that you are "using up" your lifetime Gift Tax Exclusion.

Some of the problems associated with an outright gift may be avoided by transferring the property to your child while keeping a Life Estate for yourself. For example, you should be able to keep to keep your Homestead Tax Credit if you have a Life Estate in the property (RCW 84.36.381). But, there are still tax issues and concerns regarding shared control of the property. As with joint ownership, you will not be able to sell or transfer the property during your lifetime unless your child agrees to the transfer. And as with joint ownership, should you sell the property your child is entitled to some part of the proceeds of the sale.

Before making any real property transfer, it is important to consult with your accountant, and/or attorney, and/or financial planner, to examine all aspects related to the transfer. If you are considering transferring your homestead because of your concern for the cost of future health care, before doing so, consult with an Elder Law attorney. He will be able to suggest ways to protect your assets, and still ensure that you receive the health care that you may require in your later years.

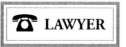 **LAWYER**   OUT OF STATE PROPERTY

Each state is in charge of the way property located in that state is transferred. If you own property in another state (or country) then you need to consult with an attorney in that state (or country) to determine how that property will be transferred to your beneficiaries once you die. Most state laws are similar to Washington, namely, property held as Joint Tenants With Right of Survivorship or a Life Estate Interest can be transferred without the need for Probate.

If you own property in another state in your name only, or as a Tenant In Common, or if you hold property jointly with your spouse in a community property state, then a Probate procedure may need to be held in that state. If it is necessary to have a Probate procedure in Washington, then a second Probate procedure may need to be held in the state where the property is located. This could have the effect of doubling the cost of Probate.

Still another problem is the matter of taxes. Inheritance taxes may be due in the state where the property is held. It may be necessary to file a tax return in two states. In addition to increased taxes, this can double the cost of the accounting fees.

You may wish to consult with an attorney for suggestions about how to set up your Estate Plan to avoid such problems.

A full Probate procedure may be necessary if you hold personal property in your name only that is worth more than $60,000. Probate will be necessary to transfer real property held in your name only, regardless of the value of that property. We explored different ways to re-title property to avoid Probate, but these methods may have trade-offs that are unacceptable to you. One way to avoid many of these potential problems is to set up a *Revocable Living Trust* (also known as an *Inter Vivos Trust*).

A Revocable Living Trust is designed to care for your property during your lifetime and then to distribute your property once you die without the need for Probate. You may have been encouraged to set up such a Trust by your financial planner, or attorney, or accountant. Even people of modest means are being encouraged to use a Trust as the basis of their Estate Plan. But Trusts also have their pros and cons. Before getting into that, let's first discuss what a Trust is and how it works:

SETTING UP A TRUST

To create a Trust, an attorney prepares the Trust document in accordance with the client's needs and desires. The person who signs the document is called the *Trustor* or *Settlor.* If the *Trustor* also funds the Trust, then he is also referred to as the *Grantor.* We will refer to the Revocable Living Trust as the "Living Trust" or just the "Trust" and the person setting up the Trust as the "Grantor." The Trust document identifies who is to be the Trustee (manager) of property placed in the Trust. Usually the Grantor appoints himself as Trustee so that he is in total control of property that he places into the Trust. The Trust document also names a Successor Trustee who will take over the management of the Trust property should the Trustee resign, or become disabled or die.

Once the Trust document is properly signed, the Grantor transfers property into the Trust. The Grantor does this by changing the name on the account from his individual name to his name as Trustee. For example, if Elaine Richards sets up a Trust naming herself as Trustee, and she wishes to place her bank account into the Trust then all she need do is instruct the bank to change the name on the account from ELAINE RICHARDS to:

ELAINE RICHARDS, TRUSTEE of the ELAINE RICHARDS REVOCABLE TRUST AGREEMENT DATED JULY 12, 2001.

When the change is made, all the money in the account becomes Trust property. Elaine (wearing her Trustee hat) has total control of the account, taking money out and putting money in as she sees fit. Similarly, if she wants to put real property into the Trust all she need do is have her attorney prepare a new deed with the Grantee identified as ELAINE RICHARDS, TRUSTEE.

The Trust document states how the Trust property is to be managed during Elaine's lifetime. Should Elaine become disabled the Trust will provide for her Successor Trustee to take over and manage the Trust property. Because the Trust is revocable, if she wishes, Elaine can terminate the Trust at any time and have all the Trust property placed back into her own individual name. If she does not revoke her Trust during her lifetime, then once she dies the Trust becomes irrevocable, and her Successor Trustee must follow the terms of the Trust Agreement as written. If the Trust says to give the Trust property to certain beneficiaries, the Successor Trustee will do so; and in most cases without any Probate procedure. If the Trust directs the Successor Trustee to continue to hold property in Trust and use the money to take care of a member of Elaine's family, then the Successor Trustee will do so.

THE GOOD PART

Setting up a Trust has many good features.

☆☆ AVOID PROBATE

In Washington, Probate can be time consuming and very expensive. Both the Personal Representative and his attorney are entitled to payment for their services. These fees can be significant. It may be necessary to hire accountants and appraisers, as well. If you have property in two states, then two Probate procedures may be necessary (one in each state) and that could have the effect of doubling the cost of Probate. If the Trust is properly drafted and your property placed into the Trust, you should be able to avoid Probate altogether.

☆ CARE FOR FAMILY MEMBER

You can make provision in your Trust to care for a minor child or family member after you die. If your family member is immature or a born spender, you can set up a *Spendthrift Trust* to protect him/her from squandering the inheritance. You can direct your Successor Trustee to use Trust funds to pay for the family member's living expenses, education, health care and nothing more. The Trust can be set up so that the Trust property is protected from the creditors of the beneficiary (RCW 6.32.250).

NO CREDITOR PROTECTION FOR GRANTOR

Property you place in your Revocable Living Trust is freely accessible to you. It is likewise accessible to your creditors both before and after your death. If you die owing money, your creditors can have a Personal Representative appointed to locate funds to pay those debts. The Personal Representative can require that your Trust property be used to pay for those debts (RCW 11.18.200, 19.36.020).

☆☆ AVOID APPOINTMENT OF A GUARDIAN

Once you have a Trust you do not need to worry about who will take care of your property should you become disabled or too aged to handle your finances. The person you appoint as Successor Trustee will take over the care of the Trust property if you are unable to do so. If you do not make provision for the care of your property, it may be necessary for a Court to appoint a Guardian of your property. Guardianship is a good thing to avoid, not only because of the cost of the procedure, but also to avoid the embarrassment of a Court coming to the conclusion that you are not competent to manage your own finances.

Before appointing a Guardian, the Court will have a hearing to determine whether you competent to manage your property. You are entitled to your own attorney at the hearing. If you do not have one the Court can appoint an attorney for you. If the Court determines that you do not have the capacity to handle your finances, he will appoint a Guardian. The Court may order the Guardian to obtain a bond for the protection of your property. Once appointed, the Guardian will take possession of your property and file an inventory with the Court. The Guardian will manage your property and each year account to the Court for monies spent. He may need to employ an accountant to assist with these reports. The Guardian needs to employ an attorney to establish the Guardianship and see that it is properly administered. The Guardian, and his attorney are entitle to be paid for their efforts on your behalf (RCW 11.88.010, 11.88.045, 11.88.100, 11.92.040).

Court filing fees, the cost of a bond, accounting fees, Guardian's fees, attorney's fees for you and the Guardian, are all paid from your Estate (that's your money!). And this expense goes on year after year until you are restored to capacity or die.

☆ PRIVACY

Your Living Trust is a private document. No one but your Trustee and your beneficiaries need ever read it. If you leave property in a Will and there is a Probate procedure, the Will must be filed with the court, where it becomes a public document (RCW 36.23.030). Anyone can go to the courthouse, read your Will and see who you did (or did not) provide for in your Will. Records in the Probate Court (inventories, creditor's claims, etc.) are open to public scrutiny. It is not much of a stretch to predict that in the future, Court records will be available on the Internet!

LEASE SAFE DEPOSIT BOX AS TRUSTEE

As explained in Chapter 3, if you hold the safe deposit box in your name only, once the bank learns of your death, access to the box is restricted. No one will be able to gain entry to the box until a Personal Representative is appointed. And under Washington law, there is no Right of Survivorship with a joint tenant of the safe deposit box, so once the bank learns of your death, they will not allow a joint tenant to remove items from the box (RCW 11.02.130).

One of the benefits of having a Living Trust is that you can lease the safe deposit box in your name as Trustee, making the contents of the safe deposit box, Trust property. You can lease the box jointly with your Successor Trustee. This protects your privacy. By leasing a safe deposit box as Trustee, only you and your Successor Trustee need ever know of the contents of the box.

☆ ESTATE TAX SAVINGS

Many people think that the Estate Tax will be phased out so that by 2010, no Estate Taxes will be due regardless of the size of an Estate. But under current law in 2011, the Estate Tax is scheduled to be reinstated and estates worth more than $1,000,000 will once again be subject to a sizeable Estate Tax. A couple with an Estate in excess of a million dollars can reduce the risk of an Estate Tax by setting up his and her Trusts, so that each person can take advantage of his own Estate Tax Exclusion value. For example, if a couple own 2 million dollars, they can set up a Trust so that separate their funds into two Trusts each valued at one million dollars. Each Trust can be set up so that a surviving spouse can use the income from the deceased partner's Trust for living expenses. In this way, their standard of living need not be reduced by separating their funds into two Trusts.

If they do not wish to separate funds, they can set up a single Joint Trust that separates into two Trusts once one partner dies. Again, the surviving spouse is free to use the income from both Trusts. Once both partners are deceased, the beneficiaries of their respective Trusts will inherit the funds, hopefully with no Estate Tax due. If the couple do not set up his/her Trusts and continue to hold their property jointly, then the last to die will own the two million dollars with only one Estate Tax Exclusion available.

With all these perks, you may be ready to call your attorney to make an appointment to set up a Trust, but before doing so there are a few things you need to consider.

THE PROBLEMS

⊠   COMPLEXITY

A Trust is a fairly complex document, often 20 pages long. It needs to be that long because you are establishing a vehicle for taking care of your property during your lifetime, as well as after your death. The Trust usually is written in "legalese," so it may take you considerable time and effort to understand it. It is important to have your Trust document prepared by an attorney who has the patience to work with you until you fully understand each paragraph of the document and are satisfied that this is what you want.

⊠   PROBATE MIGHT STILL BE NECESSARY

The Trust only works for those items that you place in the Trust. If you purchase a security in your name only, and without a "Transfer On Death" designation into your Trust, or to a beneficiary of your choice, a Probate procedure may be necessary to determine who should inherit that security. The attorney who prepares your Trust usually creates a safety net for such a situation by having you sign a *Pour Over Will* at the same time you sign your Trust. The purpose of the Will is to "pour" any asset titled in your name only, into the Trust; specifically, the Will directs your Personal Representative to put any asset held in your name only into your Trust (RCW 11.12.250).

This ensures that all of your property will go to the beneficiaries named in your Trust. But the downside is that a full Probate procedure may be necessary to get the asset into the Trust. This defeats a major goal of the Trust, namely to avoid Probate. You can ensure that a Probate procedure will not be necessary by transferring your assets into your Trust during your lifetime, but if you forget to put something into your Trust, the Pour Over Will stands by to transfer that asset into your Trust.

⊠ COST

Because of the thoroughness of the document and the fact that it is custom designed for you, a Trust will cost much more to draft than a simple Will. In addition to the initial cost of the Trust, it can be expensive to maintain the Trust should you become disabled or die. Your Successor Trustee has the right to charge for his duties as Trustee, as well as for any specialized service he performs. For example, if you choose an attorney to be Successor Trustee, the attorney has the right to charge to manage the Trust, and also to charge for any legal work he performs. A financial institution can charge to serve as Successor Trustee, and also charge to manage the Trust portfolio.

You could appoint a family member who may serve as Successor Trustee for little or no compensation. But regardless of whether you choose a professional or a family member to be Successor Trustee, you need to come to a written agreement as to what will be charged to manage the Trust. The fee agreement can be included in the Trust document with a provision that whoever accepts the job of Successor Trustee, agrees to accept the fee as provided in the Trust document.

If you do not make written provision for fees, then under Washington law, the Trustee (and his attorney) are entitled to charge a reasonable fee and to charge that fee to the Trust (RCW 11.104.130). If the beneficiaries of the Trust think the fee unreasonable, their only recourse is to employ their own attorney and bring the matter before the Court. As explained on the previous page, the Trustee can spend Trust funds to defend his right to reasonable compensation. No matter what the outcome, the beneficiaries will inherit just that much less because of the dispute.

⊠ YOU MAY NEED YOUR SPOUSE'S PERMISSION TO TRANSFER PROPERTY INTO YOUR TRUST

If you are married, you have the right to transfer your separate property into the Trust, but you will need written authority from your spouse to transfer Community Property into the Trust (RCW 26.16.030). This also applies to Quasi-community Property. In fact, if within 3 years of your death, you make a gift of out of state property without permission from your spouse, your spouse has the right to require the beneficiary of that gift to return half of the value of that property to your Estate (RCW 26.16.240).

⊠ TAXES MAY STILL BE A PROBLEM

While you are operating the Trust as Trustee, all of the property held in your Revocable Living Trust is taxed as if you were holding that property in your own name. If the value of your Trust property exceeds the Estate and/or Gift Tax Exclusion value, taxes will be due and owing once you die. For those in that fortunate tax bracket, an experienced financial planner or tax attorney can suggest other, more advanced, Estate Planning strategies to reduce taxes.

⊠ ☆ THE TRUST IS LEGALLY ENFORCEABLE

Any beneficiary, or Trustee, of the Trust can petition the Superior Court to settle a dispute arising out of the administration of the Trust (RCW 11.98.039). We gave this section a cross and a star, because the right to have a Trust enforced or administered by a court is a double edged sword. It is great to have a court protect the rights of your beneficiaries, but the cost of a court battle could be greater than if your Estate was subject to Probate in the first place.

Worse yet, your beneficiaries are at a disadvantage because the Trustee can charge the legal expenses to your Trust, while the beneficiaries must pay for their legal battles out of their own pocket. Even if the beneficiaries win the argument, the Trustee's legal fees are paid from the Trust, so there is just that much less to inherit.

Although all of the methods discussed in this Chapter can be used to transfer property without the need for Probate, it may be each method has a downside that is objectionable to you. Maybe you don't have enough money to warrant the cost of setting up the Trust at this time. Holding property jointly with another may raise issues of security and independence. Holding property so that it goes directly to a few beneficiaries in a POD, TOD, or ITF account, may not be as flexible as you wish. This is especially the case if you wish to give gifts to several charities or to minor children instead of just one or two beneficiaries. For example, if you hold all your property so that it goes to your son without the need for Probate, and you ask him to use some of the money for your grandchild's education, it may be that your grandchild gets none of the money because your son is sued or falls upon hard times. If you keep your property in your name only and leave a Will giving a certain amount of money for your grandchild, then the child will know exactly how much money you left and the purpose of that gift.

After taking into account all the pros and cons of avoiding Probate, you may well opt for a Will and a Probate procedure. If you make such a decision, it is important to keep in mind that Estate Planning is not an "all or nothing" choice. You can arrange your Estate so that certain items pass automatically to your intended beneficiary, and other items can be left in your name only, to be distributed as part of a Probate procedure. By arranging your finances in this manner, you can reduce the value of your Probate Estate, and that in turn should reduce the cost of Probate.

Your Washington Will

Many people decide that the Will is the best route to go but do not act upon it, thinking it unnecessary to prepare a Will until they are very old and about to die. But according to reports published by the National Center for Health Statistics (a division of the U.S. Department of Health and Human Services) 2 of every 10 people who die in any given year are under the age of 60.

Twenty percent may seem like a small number until it hits close to home as it did with a young couple. The couple was having difficulty conceiving a child. They went from doctor to doctor until they met someone just beginning his practice. With his knowledge of the latest advances in medicine, he was able to help them.

The birth of their child was a moment of joy and gratitude. They asked a nurse to take a picture of them all together — the proud parents, the newborn child and the doctor who made it all possible. Happiness radiated from the picture, but within 6 months, one of them would be dead.

You might think it was the child. An infant's life is so fragile. SIDS and all manner of childhood diseases can threaten a little one. But no, he grew up a healthy young man.

If you looked at the picture, you might guess the husband. Overweight and stressed out; his ruddy complexion suggested high blood pressure. He looked like a typical heart-attack-prone type A personality.

No, he was fine and went on to enjoy raising his son.

Probably the wife. She had such a difficult time with the pregnancy and the delivery was especially hard. Perhaps it was all too much for her. No, she recovered and later had two more children.

It was the doctor who was killed in a collision with a truck.

WHY A WILL IS NECESSARY

Though we all agree that one never knows, still people put off making a Will figuring that if they die before getting around to it, Washington law will take over and their property will be distributed in the manner that they would have wanted anyway. The problem with that logic is the complexity of the Washington's Laws of Descent and Distribution. If you are survived by a spouse, child, parent or sibling, then it isn't too difficult to figure out who will inherit your property. But if none of these survive you, the ultimate beneficiary of your property may not be the person you would have chosen, had you taken the time to do so.

Others think that it is not necessary to have a Will because they have arranged their finances so that all of their property will be inherited without the need for Probate. But money could come into your Estate after your death. This could happen in any number of ways from winning the lottery and dying (of happiness, no doubt) to receiving insurance funds after your death. For example, if you die in a house fire or flood the insurance company may need to pay for damage done to your property. In such case, a Personal Representative may need to be appointed and the monies distributed according to Washington law.

If you die without a Will, the Personal Representative may not be the person you would have chosen. The monies may be distributed differently than you would have wished. And there are other important reasons to make a Will.

MAKE GIFTS OF YOUR PERSONAL PROPERTY

Another benefit to making a Will is that you can make provision for who will get your personal property, including your car. If you make a gift of your car in your Will, then it will be relatively simple for your car to be transferred to the beneficiary. If you do not make a specific gift of your car, it becomes part of your Probate Estate. Your Personal Representative will decide what to do with the car. He can sell it and include the proceeds of the sale in the Estate funds to be distributed to your residuary beneficiaries; or he can give the car to one beneficiary of your Estate as part of that beneficiary's share of the Estate.

SMALL GIFTS MATTER

Many who have lost someone close to them report that the distribution of personal effects (clothing, jewelry, photo albums, etc.) caused the greatest conflict. If you arrange your finances so that no Probate procedure is necessary, your next of kin will need to decide, between themselves, how your personal effects should be distributed. Without guidance from you and no Personal Representative with authority to make decisions, there could be much disagreement and hard feelings, over items of little monetary value.

If you make a Will, you can include a list in your Will of who is to receive your personal effects. Your Personal Representative will distribute your personal effects according to that list. Under Washington statute 11.12.260 if you refer to the list in your Will and you clearly describe the item and who is to receive it, then your Personal Representative will distribute the property according to that list. The statute does not allow money, bank accounts, securities or a mobile home to be distributed as part of a list. Those items need to be included as part of the Will itself.

Washington statute 11.12.260 does allow you to include cars, boats, and airplanes in the list, but the better form is to include those items in your Will and reserve the list for just those items with more sentimental, than monetary value.

Of course, you cannot make provision in your Will for each and every personal item you own. But you can instruct your Personal Representative to allow certain family members to take their choice of items not mentioned in your Will; and to use an appropriate lottery system to distribute items requested by two or more family members.

 YOU CAN'T GIVE WHAT YOU DON'T HAVE

It is a good idea to keep your list updated. You could lose or give away a personal item on the list. Unless you substitute a different gift, that beneficiary is out of luck. Also, if you are married, then you can only include personal items that are your own Separate Property. Your surviving spouse owns half of all of your Community Property, and in most cases, it will be impossible to give away half of a personal item that is Community Property. For example, if your personal computer is Community Property, it makes no sense to give away your "half."

And if you have a Community Property Agreement, then all of the items covered in that Agreement are spoken for. You cannot make any other provision for those items because upon your death, they will go to your surviving spouse. In a way, the Community Property Agreement operates like a Will, but unlike a Will it cannot be changed unless both your and your spouse sign a new Agreement (RCW 26.16.120).

📄 MAKE ADJUSTMENT FOR PRIOR GIFTS

You can make adjustments in your Will for gifts or loans given during your lifetime. For example, if you loan money to a family member and do not expect to be repaid, you can deduct the loan from that person's inheritance. There is no need to make the adjustment if the borrower gives you a promissory note because should you die, the monies will be owed to your Estate and the Personal Representative can deduct the monies owed from the borrower's inheritance. But if there is no evidence of the debt and you neglect to make a Will, the borrower will receive whatever is allowed under Washington's Laws of Descent and Distribution (RCW 11.04.041).

That was the case with Sally and Tom and their four children. They were firm believers in treating each of their children equally. "Share and share alike" was their favorite saying. Once Tom died, Sally continued with the tradition.

Sally did not think of the loan she gave to her son as a gift. After all, he promised to pay it back, with interest! She did not ask her son to sign a promissory note. He was family. If you can't trust your son, who can you trust?

The son was prompt with his monthly payments. But only two payments were made prior to his mother's untimely death from a heart attack.

Sally never mentioned the loan to any of her other children. Neither did her son. Each child received one-quarter of their mother's Estate; and none the wiser.

Except whenever Sally's son dreams of his mother, she is not smiling.

APPOINT A PERSONAL REPRESENTATIVE

An important reason to make a Will is so that you can choose your own Personal Representative. If you are married, you need to keep in mind that your surviving spouse has the right to serve as Personal Representative over all of your Community Property. If you choose someone other than your surviving spouse, then that person can only administer your separate property. If you name someone other that your surviving spouse as Executor, the Court could appoint two Personal Representatives, your spouse for your Community Property and your Executor for your Separate Property. This could significantly increase the cost of probating your Estate.

PROVIDE FOR A SUPERVISED ADMINISTRATION

As explained Chapter 6, the Probate procedure can be supervised by the Probate Court, or the Court can grant your Personal Representative Nonintervention Powers. It is less expensive to administer an Estate when the Personal Representative can operate independently; and that is surely the way to go if you are leaving your all of your property to the Personal Representative, or to two people who you appoint as Co-Personal Representative. But if you are leaving your property to several beneficiaries you need to consider whether you want the Court to supervise the actions of your Personal Representative. If you want the administration to be supervised, then you need leave directions in your Will saying that the Court shall supervise the administration and shall not grant Noninterventions Powers. If you make no mention in your Will one way or the other, it will be up to your beneficiaries to decide whether they want Court supervision or whether they will allow the Court to grant Nonintervention powers (RCW 11.68.011).

ARRANGE FOR PERSONAL REPRESENTATIVE FEES

You can make provision in your Will for the amount of money your Personal Representative should receive for performing his duties to administer your Estate. You need to be sure that this amount is agreeable to the Personal Representative, because under Washington law, he can accept the amount provided in your Will or, before he is appointed as Personal Representative, he can renounce all claim to that compensation, and ask the Court to decide how much he should receive (RCW 11.48.210).

One way to avoid the problem is to have a compensation agreement signed by your Personal Representative attached to your Will. By signing the Agreement, your Personal Representative is promising to accept the fee as provided in the Will. Having a separate fee agreement will not stop your Personal Representative from renouncing the amount provided in the Will; but with such an agreement, the Court will not agree to increase the amount agreed upon except under extraordinary circumstances. Also keep in mind that the Personal Representative's fee is just to administer the Estate. It does not include payment for professional work he may do while administering the Estate. If you decide to choose a professional to serve as Personal Representative (attorney, accountant, financial planner, etc.), then have your compensation agreement include what he will be paid for professional duties he performs as part of the administration of the Estate.

CHOOSE A GUARDIAN FOR A MINOR CHILD

Each parent has the right to name someone in their Will to be Guardian of their minor child in the event that the parent dies before the child is grown, and the other parent is deceased or unable to care for the child. When appointing a Guardian, the Probate Court will give priority to the person of your choice (RCW 11.88.080).

Some people think that preparing a Will is a simple thing — something they can do themselves. But preparing a Will is like figure skating. It is harder than it looks. A Will needs to be clearly worded. A sentence that can be read in two different ways can lead to a dispute over what you intended; and that could result in a long and expensive Court battle. The Will must be signed and witnessed according to Washington law, otherwise the Judge may refuse to admit the Will to Probate, and your property will be distributed as if you had no Will at all.

Unless you take the time to make yourself knowledgable about Washington law as it relates to Wills, it is best to have an attorney who is experienced in Estate Planning, prepare one for you.

STORING THE WILL

Once you sign your Will, you may wonder where to store it. Your attorney may suggest that he place it in his vault for safekeeping. By doing so, he ensures that your heirs will need to contact him as soon as you die. This does not mean that they are required to employ him should a Probate proceeding be necessary. It only means that he will have an opportunity for future employment. In exchange, he gives you a good value. Your Will is kept safely in his vault, and at sole cost to him.

Before allowing your attorney to store the Will, you need assurance that the attorney will be responsible for the document. You should get a receipt and something in writing that says:

⇨   There will be no charge to you, or your heirs, for the storage and retrieval of the document.

⇨ The attorney accepts full responsibility for the storage of the Will. Should it be lost or damaged, he will replace the document at no cost to you; and if you are deceased, he will, at no cost to your heirs, present sufficient evidence to the Court to accept a valid copy of the Will into Probate.

With all of this cost and liability, many attorneys will agree only to store a copy of your Will. In such case, you can keep the document in a fireproof safe deposit box within your home; and give a duplicate key to the person you have chosen to be your Personal Representative.

THE SAFE DEPOSIT BOX — SAFE BUT . . .
You might consider placing your Will in a safe deposit box that you lease at a bank. The only problem with the bank safe deposit box is convenient access. If you hold a safe deposit box in your name only, should you die, the bank will restrict access to the safe deposit box. It may take a Court order to inspect the contents of the box. But if you arranged your finances to avoid Probate, then it is self defeating to have entry to a safe deposit box trigger a Court procedure.

As explained earlier in this Chapter, those who have a Trust can solve the problem by giving their Successor Trustee joint access to the safe deposit box. If you do not have a Trust consider leasing the box jointly with a trusted family member. Of course, if privacy and security are important to you, then this might offset any concern for the convenience of your beneficiaries.

Regardless of where you choose to store your Will, let your Personal Representative know that you have a Will and how to retrieve it in the event of your death.

CHOOSING THE RIGHT ESTATE PLAN

Joint Ownership?
An "In Trust For" account?
A POD account?
A TOD security?
A Trust?
A Community Property Agreement?
A Will?
An Insurance Policy???

This chapter offers so many options that the reader may be more confused than when he was blissfully unenlightened.

As with most things in life, you may find there are no ultimate solutions, just alternatives. The right choice for you is the one that best accomplishes your goal. This being the case, you first need to determine what you want to accomplish with the money you leave. Think about what will happen to your property if you were to die suddenly, without making any plan different from the one you now have.   Who will get your property?
                    Will any tax need to be paid?
                    Will Probate be necessary?

If the answers to these questions are not what you wish, then you need to work to retitle your property to accomplish your goals.

For those with significant assets, especially those with Estates large enough to pay Estate taxes, a trip to an experienced Estate Planning attorney may be well worth the consultation fee.

Your Estate Plan Record 9

Once you are satisfied with your Estate Plan, then the final thing to consider is whether your heirs will be able to locate your assets once you are deceased.

Most people have their business records in one place, their Will in another place, car titles and deeds in still another place. When someone dies, their beneficiaries may feel as if they are playing a game of "hide and seek" with the decedent. The game might be fun were it not for the fact that an unlocated item may be forever lost. For example, suppose you die in an accident and no one knows you are insured by your credit card company for accidental death in the amount of $25,000. The only one to profit is the insurance company, which is just that much richer because no one told them that you died as a result of an accident.

And how about a key to a safe deposit box located in another state? Will anyone find it? Even if they find the key, how will they find the box?

It is not difficult to arrange things so that your affairs are always in order. It amounts to being aware of what you own (and owe) and keeping a record of your possessions. A side benefit is that by doing so, you will always know where all your business records are. If you ever spent time trying to collect information to file your taxes or trying to find a lost stock or bond certificate, you will appreciate the value of organizing your records.

ORGANIZING YOUR RECORDS

Heirs need all the help they can get. It is difficult enough dealing with the loss, without the frustration of trying to locate important documents. Your heirs will have no problem locating your assets if you keep all of your records in a single place. It can be a desk drawer or a file cabinet or even a shoe box. It is helpful if you keep a separate file or folder for each type of investment. You might consider setting up the following folders:

📁 THE BANK & SECURITIES FOLDER

Store your original certificates for stocks, bonds, mutual funds, certificates of deposit, in a folder labeled BANK & SECURITIES FOLDER. In addition to the original certificate include a copy of the contract you signed with each financial institution. The contract will show where you have funds and who you named as beneficiary or joint owner of the account. If someone owes you money and has signed a promissory note or mortgage that identifies you as the lender, then you can store these documents in this folder as well.

If you wish to store your original documents in a safe deposit box, then keep a record of the location of the safe deposit box, and the number of the box, in this folder. Make a copy of all of the items stored in the box and place the copies in this folder. If you have an extra key to the box, then put the key in the folder. If you are the only person with access to the box, it may take a Probate procedure to remove items from the box once you die. Consider allowing someone you trust to be able to gain entry to the box in the event of your incapacity or death.

📁 THE INSURANCE FOLDER

The INSURANCE FOLDER is for each insurance policy that you own, be it life insurance, car insurance, homeowner's insurance or health care insurance. If you purchased real property, you probably received a title commitment at closing and the original title insurance policy some weeks later when you received your original deed from recording. If you cannot locate the title insurance policy, then contact the closing agent and have them send you a copy of your title insurance policy.

📁 THE PENSION AND ANNUITY FOLDER

If you have a Pension or Annuity, then put all of the documents relating to the Pension in this folder. Include the telephone number and/or address of the person to contact in the event of your death.

FOR FEDERAL RETIREES If you are a Federal Retiree, you should have received your PERSONAL IDENTIFICATION NUMBER (PIN) and the person who will inherit your pension (your *survivor annuitant*) should have received his/her own PIN as well. It is relatively simple to obtain this during your lifetime, but it may be difficult and/or stressful for your survivor annuitant to work through the system once you are gone.

Survivor annuitant benefits are not automatic. Your survivor annuitant must apply for them by submitting a death claim to the Office of Personnel Management. Your survivor needs to know that it is necessary to apply and also how to apply. You can get printed information about how to apply for benefits from the Office Of Personnel Management (see Page 32) and place the information in this file.

🗀 THE DEED FOLDER

Many people save every scrap of paper associated with the closing of real property. If you closed recently on real estate and there was a mortgage involved in the purchase, you probably walked away from closing with enough paper to wallpaper your kitchen. If you wish, you can keep all of those papers in a separate file that identifies the property, for example:

CLOSING PAPERS FOR THE SPOKANE CONDO

Place the original deed (or a copy if the original is in a safe deposit box) in a separate DEED FOLDER. Include cemetery deeds, condominium deeds, cooperative shares to real property, timesharing certificates, deed to out of state property, etc. Also include a copy of related documents such as an Abstract of Title, or a recorded Condominium Approval. If you have a title insurance policy, put the original in the insurance folder, and a copy in this folder. If you have a mortgage on your property, put a copy of the recorded mortgage and promissory note in a separate LIABILITY FOLDER.

LOCATING REAL PROPERTY

If you own a vacant lot, your beneficiaries will find the deed (or a copy) in this folder but that deed will not contain the address of that property because it doesn't have one. The post office does not assign a street address until someone actually lives at the site. Your beneficiary could get the location of the property from city or county records. But why make things hard for them? Include a simple handwritten note in this folder that tells them exactly how to locate the property.

📁 THE LIABILITY FOLDER

The LIABILITY FOLDER should contain all loan documents of monies that you owe. For example, if you purchased real property and have a mortgage on that property, put a copy of the mortgage and promissory note in this folder. If you owe money on a car, put the loan documents in this folder. If you have a credit card, put a copy of the contract you signed with the credit card company in this folder.

Many people never take the time to calculate their net worth (what a person owns less what that person owes). By having a record of your assets and outstanding debts, you can calculate your net worth whenever you wish.

📁 THE ESTATE PLANNING DOCUMENT FOLDER

Place your Will and/or Trust in a separate folder. If your attorney has your original Will, then make a note of that fact together with a copy of the Will. If the original document is in a safe deposit box, then place a copy of the document in this folder together with instructions about how to find the original. It is important to keep a copy of your Will or Trust because over the years you may forget what provision you made. Keeping a copy in your home may save you a trip to the safe deposit box to determine whether you need to update the document.

If you made burial or funeral arrangements, then you can include those documents in this folder.

THE PERSONAL PROPERTY FOLDER

MOTOR VEHICLES

Put all motor vehicle titles in a Personal Property folder. This includes cars, mobile homes, boats, planes, etc. If you owe money on the vehicle, the lender may have possession of the title certificate. If such is the case, then put a copy of the title certificate and registration in this folder and a copy of the loan documents in a separate liability folder. If you have a boat or plane, then identify the location of the motor vehicle. For example, if you are leasing space in an airplane hangar or in a marina, keep a copy of the leasing agreement in this file.

JEWELRY

If you own expensive jewelry, keep a picture of the item together with the sales receipt or written appraisal in this folder.

COLLECTOR'S ITEMS

If you own a valuable art or coin collection, or any other item of significant value, include a picture of the item in this file. Also include evidence of ownership of the item, such as a sales receipt or a certificate of authenticity, or a written appraisal of the property.

🗁 THE PERSONAL RECORD FOLDER

The PERSONAL RECORDS FOLDER should include documents that relate to you personally, such as a birth certificate, naturalization papers, pre-nuptial or post- nuptial agreement, marriage certificate, divorce papers, military records, Social Security card, etc. If you have a Power of Attorney, you can place the document in this folder or in your Estate Planning folder. If you placed the original document in a safe deposit box, then keep a copy in this folder together with the location of the original.

🗁 THE TAX RECORD FOLDER

Your Personal Representative (or next of kin) will need to file your final income tax returns. Keep a copy of your tax returns (both federal and state) for the past three years in your Tax Record Folder.

As explained in Chapter 2, beginning in 2010, there will be a cap on the step-up basis to 4.3 million dollars for property inherited by the spouse and 1.3 million dollars for property inherited by anyone else. It is important to keep a record of the basis of your property, not only for your heirs, but yourself should you decide to sell the property during your lifetime. If you purchase real property, you need to keep a record of the purchase price as well as monies you paid to improve the property. You will need these records to determine whether there will be a Capital Gains Tax on the transfer. Your accountant can help you set up a bookkeeping system to keep a running record of your basis in everything you own of value.

THE *If I Die* FILE

Many do not have the time, nor inclination, to "play" with all these folders. They do not anticipate an immediate demise. Getting hit by a truck, or dying in a fiery plane crash is not something to think about, much less prepare for. But consider that death is not the only problem. You could take suddenly ill (say with a stroke) and become incapacitated. Even the most time-starved optimist should have a murmur of concern that his loved ones will be left with a mess should something unforeseen happen.

If you do not feel like doing a complete job of organizing your records at this time, consider an abridged version. You can set up a single file with a list of all you own and the location of each item. You need to make that file easily accessible to whoever you wish to manage your affairs in the event of your incapacity or death. You can do this by letting that person know of the existence of the file and how to get it in an emergency; or keep the file in an easily accessed place in your home with the succinct but attention-grabbing title of "*If I Die*."

We have included a form on the next page that you can use as a basis for information to be included in the file.

If I Die

then the following information will help settle my Estate:

INFORMATION FOR DEATH CERTIFICATE

MY FULL LEGAL NAME _____

MY SOCIAL SECURITY NO. _____

MY USUAL OCCUPATION _____

BIRTH DATE AND BIRTH PLACE _____

If naturalized, date & place _____

MY FATHER'S NAME _____

MY MOTHER'S MAIDEN NAME _____

PEOPLE TO BE NOTIFIED

_____

_____

_____

FUNERAL AND BURIAL ARRANGEMENTS

LOCATION OF BURIAL SITE

_____

LOCATION OF PREPAID FUNERAL CONTRACT

_____

FOR VETERAN or SPOUSE BURIAL IN A NATIONAL CEMETERY

BRANCH_____SERIAL NO._____

VETERAN'S RANK _____

VETERAN'S VA CLAIM NUMBER _____

DATE AND PLACE OF ENTRY INTO SERVICE:

_____

DATE AND PLACE OF SEPARATION FROM SERVICE:

_____

LOCATION OF OFFICIAL MILITARY DISCHARGE
OR DD 214 FORM_____

LOCATION OF LEGAL DOCUMENTS

BIRTH CERTIFICATE _____

MARRIAGE CERTIFICATE_____

DIVORCE DECREE _____

PASSPORT _____

WILL OR TRUST _____

DEEDS _____

MORTGAGES _____

TITLE TO MOTOR VEHICLES _____

HEALTH CARE DIRECTIVES _____

Name, telephone of attorney   _____

LOCATION OF FINANCIAL RECORDS

INSURANCE POLICIES:

Name of Company, Location of Policy, Insurance Agent

_____

_____

PENSIONS/ANNUITIES:

IF FEDERAL RETIREE: PIN NUMBER: _____

NAME OF SURVIVOR _____

SURVIVOR PIN NUMBER _____

BANK

Name and address of Bank, Account Number,
Location of Safe Deposit Box and Key

_____

_____

SECURITIES

Name and telephone number of broker

_____

TAX RECORDS FOR PAST 3 YEARS

LOCATION_____

Name and telephone number of accountant

_____

KEEPING UP TO DATE

We discussed people's natural disinclination to make an Estate Plan until they are faced with their own mortality. Many believe that they will make just one Will and then die (maybe that's why they put off making a Will). The reality is, most people who make a Will change it at least once before they die. It is important to make updates it when any of the following events take place:

✍ A CHANGE IN RELATIONSHIP

If you marry, divorce, have a child, or if a beneficiary of your Estate dies, you need to examine your Estate Plan to determine whether it needs to be revised. If you decide that your Will needs a complete revision, then it is important to have a new Will prepared. If you simply rip up the old Will, that will effectively revoke the Will. But it could happen that someone (perhaps your attorney) has a copy of the Will. If no one knows that you revoked the Will, they may think the Will is lost and then offer the copy of the Will for Probate (see page 79). If you draft a new Will, then the first paragraph should say, "I revoke all prior Wills ..."

BENEFICIARY MOVES OR DIES Most people remember to name an alternate beneficiary should one of their beneficiaries die. But how many of us remember to notify the pension plan or insurance company when a beneficiary moves? It is important that your beneficiary's address be available to those in charge of distributing funds upon your death. Many life insurance proceeds are never paid because the company cannot locate the beneficiary. The Actuarial Office of the Federal Employees' Group Life Insurance Program reported that as of October, 2001, they had over 40 million dollars in unpaid benefits, mostly Because they could not locate the beneficiary at the last given address.

✍ CHANGE IN MARITAL STATUS

If you obtain a *Dissolution of Marriage*, i.e., a divorce, there are certain changes that take place by law. For example, if you divorce and then die before you get around to changing your Will any provision that you made for your ex-spouse is revoked and your Will read as if your ex-spouse died before you. If you gave your spouse a Power of Attorney, then once you divorce that Power is revoked by law (RCW 11.12.051, 11.94.040). But it is best not to rely on the law. It is important to change all documents after a divorce. This includes deeds, insurance policies, pension plans, etc.

NOTIFY EMPLOYER

If you change your marital status (either marry or divorce) you need to tell your employer of the change so that the employer can change your status for purposes of paycheck tax deductions. If you have health insurance plan or a pension plan, that provides benefits to your spouse, then these need to be changed as well.

✍ RELOCATION TO A NEW STATE OR COUNTRY

There is no need to change your Estate Plan for a move within state. There is much to check out for a move to another state or country. Each state (and country) has its own laws relating to the inheritance of property and those laws are very different from each other. The rights of a spouse to inherit property varies significantly from state to state. There is a world of difference between the rights of a spouse in a community property state and other states. And there is even variation in the rights of a spouse from one community property state to another!

If you are married and have a Will or Trust, you need to check with an attorney to be sure that your Will or Trust cannot be challenged in the new state because you did not leave your spouse the minimum amount required by the laws of that state.

No matter where your state of residence, if you die without a Will, your Probate Estate will be distributed according to the Laws of Descent of that state. Who has the right to inherit your property in Washington may be different from who can inherit your property in another state. If you do not have a Will, then this is the time to think about who will get your property in the state of your residence.

HEALTH CARE POWER OF ATTORNEY

If you signed a **Health Care Power of Attorney** appointing someone to be your **Health Care Agent** to make your medical decisions in the event you are too ill to do so yourself, you need to determine whether your Washington Health Care Power of Attorney will be honored in the new state. Laws relating to health care vary significantly. Other states may not have laws providing for the appointment of a Health Care Agent, but they may have laws that enable you to appoint a *Patient Advocate* or a *Health Care Surrogate* or a *Health Care Representative* who can make your health care decisions. It is best to sign a new document using the form and terminology recognized in that state, rather than chance any confusion should you become ill and find yourself in an emergency situation.

When moving to another state you need to either educate yourself about the laws of the state, or consult with an attorney who can assist you in reviewing your Estate Plan to see if that plan will accomplish your goals in that state.

TAXES IN NEW STATE
You also need to check out the taxes of the new state. Each state has its own Estate Tax structure. Some states have an inheritance tax, or a transfer tax on all inherited property. If state taxes are high, you may need an Estate Plan that will minimize the impact of those taxes. Creditor protection is another item that is significantly different state to state. If you have much debt, then determine what items can be inherited by your family free of your debts.

CREDITOR PROTECTION
Creditor protection is another item that is significantly different state to state. If you have much debt, then determine what items can be inherited by your family free of your debts.

✍ A SIGNIFICANT CHANGE IN THE LAW
We pay our legislators (state and federal) to make laws and, if necessary, change those in effect. We pay judges to interpret the law and that interpretation may change the way the law operates. The legislature and the judiciary do their job and so laws change frequently. Tax laws are particularly volatile. The 2001 change in the federal Estate Tax law gradually increases the Exclusion Amount so that by 2010 no federal Estate Tax will be due regardless of the value of your Estate. You may be thinking that there is no need for an Estate Tax plan because you don't intend to die prior to 2010. But any certainty relating to death and taxes is false security (especially taxes, in this case). As explained in Chapter 2, the law as passed in 2001, is effective only until December 31, 2010. If lawmakers do nothing, then on January 1, 2011, the federal Estate Tax goes back into effect; and Estates that exceed one million dollars will once again be subject to Estate taxes.

And that is not the only uncertainty. Each state has its own Estate Tax structure. It remains to be seen how each state will react to the federal change. Some states may follow the lead of the federal government and increase their Estate Tax Exclusion in the same manner. Other states may see this as an opportunity to "pick up the slack" i.e., to increase their Estate Taxes, so that monies that would have been paid to the federal government will now be paid to the state.

You need to keep up with the news to learn about changes in the law that affect your Estate Plan. It is a good idea to check with your attorney on a regular basis to see if any change in the state or federal law affects your current Estate plan. And also check out the Eagle Publishing Company Web site for changes we will post to keep this book fresh.   http://www.eaglepublishing.com

GAMES DECEDENTS PLAY

We discussed the game of "hide and seek" some decedents play with their heirs. A variation of that game is the "wild goose chase." The person who plays this game is one who never updates his files. His records are filled with all sorts of lapsed insurance policies, promissory notes of debts long since paid; brokerage statements of securities that have been sold, and so on.

When he is gone, his family will become frustrated as they try to hunt down the "missing" asset. If you wish to play this game, then the best joke is to keep the key to a safe deposit box that you are no longer leasing. That will keep folks hunting for a long time!

If you do not have a wicked sense of humor, then do your family a favor and update your records on a regular basis.

Glossary

ABSTRACT OF TITLE   An *Abstract of Title* is a condensed history of the title to the land, consisting of a summary of all of documents recorded with the County Auditor or the Recorder's Office that affect the land, including mortgages and contracts for deed.

ADMINISTRATION The *administration* of a Probate Estate is the management and settlement of the decedent's affairs. There are different types of administration. See *Ancillary Administration.*

AFFIANT   An *Affiant* is someone who signs an affidavit and swears that it is true in the presence of a notary public or other person with authority to administer an oath.

AFFIDAVIT   An *Affidavit* is a written statement of fact made by someone voluntarily and under oath, in the presence of a notary public or someone else who has authority to administer an oath.

AGENT   An *Agent* is someone who is authorized by another (the principal) to act for or in place of the principal.

ANATOMICAL GIFT   An *anatomical gift* is the donation of all or part of the body of the decedent for the purpose of transplantation or research.

ANCILLARY ADMINISTRATION An *Ancillary Administration* is a probate procedure that aids or assists the original (primary) probate proceeding. It is conducted in another state to determine the beneficiary of the decedent's property located within that state, and to determine whether the property is taxable in that state.

223

ANNUITANT   An *annuitant* is someone who is entitled to receive payments under an annuity contract.

ANNUITY   An *annuity* is a contract that gives someone (the annuitant) the right to receive periodic payments (monthly, quarterly) for the life of the annuitant or for a given number of years.

ASSET   An *asset* is anything owned by someone that has a value, including personal property (jewelry, paintings, securities, cash, motor vehicles, etc.) and real property (condominiums, vacant lots, acreage, residences, etc.)

BASIS   The *basis* is a value that is assigned to an asset for the purpose of determining the gain (or loss) on the sale of the item or in determining the value of the item in the hands of someone who has received it as a gift.

BENEFICIARY   A *beneficiary* is one who benefits from the act of another or from the transfer of property. In this book we refer to a beneficiary as someone named in a Will or Trust to receive property, or someone who inherits property under the Laws of Descent and Distribution.

BY REPRESENTATION   *By Representation* is a method of distributing property to a group of people such that if one of them dies before the gift is made, the deceased person's share goes to his/her descendants.

CAPITAL GAINS TAX   A *Capital Gains tax* is a tax on the increase in the basis of property sold by a taxpayer.

CAVEAT   *Caveat* is Latin for "Let him beware." It is a warning for the reader to be careful.

CLAIM A *Claim* against the decedent's estate is a demand for payment of a debt of the decedent. To be effective, the claim must be filed with the Probate court within the time limits set by law.

CODE A *Code* is a body of laws arranged systematically for easy reference, e.g. the Washington Revised Code.

COLUMBARIUM A *Columbarium* is a vault with niches (spaces) for urns that contain the ashes of cremated bodies.

COMMON LAW MARRIAGE A *Common Law marriage* is one that is entered into without a state marriage license or any kind of official marriage ceremony. A common law marriage is created by an agreement to marry, followed by the two living together as man and wife. Most states do not recognize a common law marriage.

COMMUNITY PROPERTY Certain states (Arizona, California, Idaho, Louisiana, Nevada, New Mexico, Texas, Washington, Wisconsin) have laws stating that property acquired by husband or wife, or both, during their marriage is *community property* and is owned equally by both of them (see Separate Property).

COMMUNITY PROPERTY AGREEMENT A *Community Property Agreement* is a written agreement between a husband and wife providing for the transfer of Community Property upon the death of one of the parties. If the Community Property Agreement is properly prepared, signed and recorded, no Probate procedure will be necessary to transfer Community Property, located in Washington, to the surviving spouse.

COURT The *Court* as used in this book is the Court that handles Probate matters. In Washington, the Probate Court is a department of the Superior Court (Probate 7050). When referring to an order made by the Court then the term is synonymous with "judge," i.e., an "order of the Court" is an order made by the judge of the Court.

CREMAINS The word *Cremains* is an abbreviation of the term *cremated remains*. It is also referred to as the *ashes* of a person who has been cremated.

CONTINGENT BENEFICIARY A *Contingent Beneficiary* is an alternate beneficiary; i.e. someone who inherits if the primary beneficiary dies or loses the right to inherit.

CREDITOR A *creditor* is someone to whom a debt is owed by another person (the *debtor*).

CURTESY *Curtesy* is the right of a husband, upon the death of his wife, to a life estate in any real property she owned during their marriage, provided they had a surviving child who could inherit the property. This English Common Law has been abolished in most states.

CUSTODIAN A *Custodian* under the Washington *Transfers to Minors Act* is a person or a financial institution that accepts responsibility for the care and management of property given to a minor child.

DAMAGES *Damages* is money that is awarded by a Court as compensation to someone who has been injured by the action of another.

DECEDENT The *Decedent* is the person who died.

DESCENDANT A **Descendant** is someone who descends from a common ancestor. There are two kinds of descendants: a *lineal descendant* and a *collateral descendant*. The lineal descendant is one who descends in a straight line such as father to son to grandson. The collateral descendant is one who descends in a parallel line, such as a cousin. In this book, unless otherwise stated, the term *descendant* refers to a *lineal descendant*.

DISTRIBUTION The **distribution** of a Probate Estate or a Trust Estate is the giving to the beneficiary that part of the estate to which the beneficiary is entitled.

DOWER **Dower** is the right of a wife, upon the death of her husband, to a Life Estate in one-third of all real property that he owned during their marriage. This English Common Law has been abolished in most states.

DURABLE POWER OF ATTORNEY A **Durable Power of Attorney** is a document in which the person who signs the document (the *Principal*) gives another person (his *Attorney in Fact*) authority to do certain things on behalf of the Principal. The Attorney in Fact is also referred to as the Principal's *Agent*. The word *"durable"* means that the authority of the Agent continues even if the Principal is incapacitated at the time that the Agent is acting on behalf of the Principal.

DURABLE POWER OF ATTORNEY FOR HEALTH CARE A **Durable Power of Attorney for Health Care** is a Durable Power of Attorney that gives the Attorney In Fact authority to make medical decisions for the Principal.

ENCUMBRANCE   An *encumbrance* is a claim or a lien or a liability that is attached to real property, such as a mortgage, or lease or a mechanic's lien.

EQUITABLE *Equitable* is whatever is right or just. If property is distributed to two or more people equitably, then the division is not necessarily equal, but according to the principles of justice or fairness.

ESTATE A person's *Estate* is all of the property (both real and personal property) owned by that person. The decedent's Estate may also be referred to as his *Taxable Estate* because all of the decedent's assets must be included when determining whether any Estate taxes are due after the person dies. Compare to Probate Estate.

EXECUTOR An *Executor* is someone appointed by a Will maker to carry out the directions made in the Will, and to dispose of the Will maker's property in the manner described in the Will.

FIDUCIARY A *Fiduciary* is one who holds property in trust for another or one who acts for the benefit of another.

GRANTEE The *Grantee* named in a deed is the person who receives title to the property from the grantor.

GRANTOR A *Grantor* is someone who transfers property. The grantor of a deed is the person who transfers property to a new owner (the *Grantee*). The grantor of a trust is someone who creates the trust and then transfer's property into the trust. See *Settlor*.

GUARDIAN   A *Guardian* is someone appointed by the Court to care for the person or property of a minor or for someone who has been found by the Court to be incapacitated.

HEALTH CARE AGENT   A *Health Care Agent* is someone who is appointed by another (the *Principal)* to authorize medical treatment for the Principal, in the event the Principal is to too ill to do so himself.

HEALTH CARE DIRECTIVE   A *Health Care Directive* that gives instructions about whether life support systems should be withheld in the event that the person who signs the Health Care Directive is terminally ill, or in a persistent vegetative state, and unable to speak for himself. In some states, this document is called a *Living Will.*

HEALTH CARE POWER OF ATTORNEY A *Health Care Power of Attorney* is a document in which someone (the *Principal*) gives another (his *Health Care Agent*) authority to make medical decisions on behalf of the Principal.

HEIR   An *Heir* is someone who is entitled to inherit the decedent's property according to the Laws of Descent in the event that the decedent dies without a Will.

HOMESTEAD The *homestead* is the dwelling and land owned and occupied as the owner's principal residence.

INCAPACITATED   The term *incapacitated* is used in two ways. A person is *physically incapacitated* if he lacks the ability to care for himself in some way. A person is *legally incapacitated* if a Court finds that a person is unable to care for his person or property, and in need of a Guardian.

INDIGENT   A person who is *indigent* is one who is poor and without funds.

ISSUE   *Issue* are all persons who have descended from a common ancestor; i.e. a person's lineal descendants.

INTEREST IN COMMON   An *Interest In Common* means that two or more people share an interest in the same property without rights of survivorship. It is the same as a *Tenancy In Common.*

INTER VIVOS TRUST   An *Inter Vivos Trust* (also known as a *Living Trust*) is Trust that is created and becomes effective during the lifetime of the Grantor (or Settlor) as opposed to a Trust that he includes as part of his Will to take effect upon his death.

INTESTATE   *Intestate* means not having a Will or dying without a Will. *Testate* is to have a Will or dying with a Will.

IRREVOCABLE CONTRACT   An *irrevocable contract* is a contract that cannot be revoked, withdrawn, or cancelled by any of the parties to that contract.

JOINT AND SEVERAL LIABILITY   If two or more people agree to be *jointly and severally liable* to pay a debt, then each individually agree to be responsible to pay the debt, and together they all agree to pay for the debt.

JURISDICTION   A *jurisdiction* is a territorial range of authority. It is the legal power of a court to hear and decide cases in that territory.

KEY MAN INSURANCE   *Key man insurance* is an insurance policy designed to protect a company from economic loss in the event that an important employee of the company becomes disabled or dies.

LAWS OF DESCENT AND DISTRIBUTION *The Laws of Descent and Distribution* are the laws of the state of Washington that determine who is entitled to inherit the decedent's Probate Estate should he die without a valid Will.

LEGALESE *Legalese* refers to the use of legal terms and confusing text that is used by some attorneys to draft legal documents.

LETTERS *Letters* is a document, issued by the Probate court, giving the Personal Representative authority to take possession of and to administer the Estate of the decedent.

LIEN A *Lien* is a charge against a person's property as security for a debt. The lien is evidence of the creditor's right to take the property as full or partial payment, in the event that the debtor defaults in paying the monies owed.

LIFE ESTATE A *Life Estate* interest in real property is the right to possess and occupy that property for so long as the holder of the life estate lives.

LITIGATION *Litigation* is the process of carrying on a lawsuit, i.e., to sue for some right or remedy in a court of law. A Litigation Attorney is one who is experienced in conducting the law suit and in particular, going to trial.

MEDICAID *Medicaid* is a public assistance program sponsored jointly by the federal and state government to provide medical care for people with low income.

MORAL TURPITUDE *Moral turpitude* is an act or behavior that gravely violates the moral standards of the community.

are paid.

NET PROBATE ESTATE The *Net Probate Estate* is the value of the decedent's Probate Estate, less all the monies paid to settle the Estate, i.e. what is left once all valid claims and the costs and expenses of the Probate procedure

NET PROCEEDS The *net proceeds* of a sale is the sale price less costs and expenses paid to make the sale.

NET WORTH A person's *net worth* is the value of all of the property that he owns less the monies he owes.

NEXT OF KIN *Next of kin* has two meanings in law: *next of kin* can refer to a person's nearest blood relation or it can refer to those people (not necessarily blood relations) who are entitled to inherit the property of the decedent if the decedent died without a Will.

NONINTERVENTION POWERS *Nonintervention Powers* are powers granted by the Court that allow the Personal Representative to settle the decedent's estate without Court supervision.

PERJURY *Perjury* is lying under oath. The false statement can be made as a witness in court or by signing an Affidavit. Perjury is a criminal offense.

PERSONAL EFFECTS *Personal effects* is property that is owned for one's personal use such as clothing, jewelry, books, and other items generally found in the one's home.

PERSONAL PROPERTY *Personal property* is all property owned by a person that is not real property (real estate). It includes personal effects, cars, securities, bank accounts, insurance policies, etc.

PERSONAL REPRESENTATIVE   A *Personal Representative* is someone who is appointed by the Probate court to settle the decedent's estate and to distribute whatever is left to the proper beneficiary.

PETITION A *Petition* is a formal written request to a Court asking the Court to take action or issue an order on a given matter.

POST-NUPTIAL AGREEMENT A *Post-nuptial agreement* is an agreement made by a couple after marriage to decide their respective rights in case of a dissolution or the death of a spouse

POWER OF ATTORNEY A *Power of Attorney* is a document in which the person who signs the document (the *Principal*) gives another person (his *Agent*) authority to do certain things on behalf of the Principal.

PRE-NUPTIAL AGREEMENT   A *Pre-nuptial Agreement* (also known as an *Antenuptial agreement*) is an agreement made prior to marriage whereby a couple determines how their property is to be managed during their marriage and how their property is to be divided should one die, or they later divorce.

PROBATE   *Probate* is a Court procedure in which a Court determines the existence of a valid Will. The Decedent's Estate is then settled by the Personal Representative who pays all valid claims and then distributes whatever remains to the proper beneficiary.

PROBATE ESTATE   The *Probate Estate* is that part of the decedent's estate that is subject to probate. It includes property that the decedent owned in his name only. It does not include property that was jointly held by the decedent and someone else. It does not include property held "in trust for" or "for the benefit of" someone.

QUASI-COMMUNITY PROPERTY *Quasi-community property* is property acquired by a married couple in a non-Community property state, that would have been Community property had that property been acquired by the couple in the Community property state.

REAL PROPERTY   *Real property,* also known as *real estate,* is land and anything permanently attached to the land such as buildings and fences.

REGISTERED AGENT   A *Registered Agent* of a corporation is someone who is authorized to act on behalf of the company and accept service of process in the event the company is sued.

RESIDUARY BENEFICIARY A *residuary beneficiary* of a Will is a beneficiary who is entitled to whatever is left of the Probate Estate once the specific gifts made in the Will have been distributed and once the decedent's bills, taxes and costs of Probate have been paid. If there is more than one residuary beneficiary, then they share equally in the residuary Estate, unless the Will provides for a different distribution.

RESIDUARY ESTATE   A *Residuary Estate* is that part of a Probate Estate that is left after all expenses and costs of administration have been paid and specific gifts have been distributed.

REVOCABLE LIVING TRUST   A ***Revocable Living Trust*** (also known as a *Inter Vivos Trust*) is a Trust that is created and becomes effective during the lifetime of the Settlor (or Grantor). A *revocable* Trust is one which can be amended or revoked by the Grantor or Settlor during his lifetime.

SEPARATE PROPERTY   In Washington, the term ***Separate Property*** refers to property that is owned by a married person in his/her own right. It includes property the person owned prior to marriage, as well as gifts and inheritances received by the person during the marriage.

SETTLOR   A ***Settlor*** is someone who furnishes property that is placed in a trust. If the Settlor is also the creator of the Trust, then the Settlor is also referred to as the Grantor.

SIBLING   A ***sibling*** is one of two or more people born of the same parents; i.e., a brother or a sister. Unless, otherwise noted, we used the term to include those who have only one parent in common; i.e. a half brother or a half sister.

SOLEMNIZE   To ***solemnize*** a marriage is to enter a marriage publicly, before witnesses, rather than privately as in a common law marriage.

SPENDTHRIFT   A ***Spendthrift*** is someone who spends money carelessly or wastefully or extravagantly.

SPENDTHRIFT TRUST   A ***Spendthrift Trust*** is a Trust created to provide monies to a beneficiary, and at the same time protect the Trust property from being taken by the creditors of the beneficiary.

STATUTE OF LIMITATION A *Statute of Limitation* is a federal or state law that sets maximum time periods for taking legal action. Once the time set out in the statute passes, no legal action can be taken.

STEP-UP BASIS A *step-up basis* is the value placed on property that is acquired in a taxable transaction such as inheriting or purchasing property (Internal Revenue Code 1012). The "step-up" refers to the increase in value of basis, from the basis of former owner (usually what he paid for it), to the basis of the new owner (usually the market value when the transfer is made).

SUPERIOR COURT See Court.

TENANCY BY THE ENTIRETY A *Tenancy by the Entirety* is the name of a form of ownership of real property held by a husband and wife. Each spouse is considered to own the property 100%. Washington, being a Community Property state, does not use that form of ownership.

TENANCY IN COMMON *Tenancy In Common* is a form of ownership such that each tenant owns his/her share without any claim to that share by the other tenants. Unlike a joint tenancy, there is no right of survivorship. Once a tenant in common dies, his/her share belongs to the tenant's Estate and not to the remaining owners of the property.

TESTATE *Testate* means having a Will or dying with a Will.

TITLE INSURANCE *Title Insurance* is a policy issued by a title company after searching title to the property. The insurance covers losses that result from a defect of title, such as unpaid taxes, or someone with a claim of ownership of the property.

TRUST AGREEMENT   A *Trust Agreement* is a document in which someone (the Grantor or Trustor) creates a trust and appoints a trustee to manage property placed into the trust. The usual purpose of the trust is to benefit persons or charities named by the Grantor as beneficiaries of the trust.

TRUSTEE   A *Trustee* is a person, or institution, who accepts the duty of caring for property for the benefit of another.

UNDUE INFLUENCE   *Undue influence* is pressure, influence or persuasion that overpowers a person's free will or judgment, so that a person acts according to the will or purpose of the dominating party.

WAIVER   A *waiver* is the intentional and voluntary giving up of a known right

WARRANTY DEED   A *Warranty Deed* is a deed in which the Grantor warrants (promises) that the property he is transferring has good and clear title; i.e., that no one else has rights in the property. This is different than a *Quit-claim Deed* where the Grantor says, in effect, "I am releasing any interest I have in this property to you, but I make no guarantees about anyone else's right to this property."

WRONGFUL DEATH   A *wrongful death* is a death that was caused by the willful or negligent act of a person or company.

INDEX

WEB SITES

STATE OF WASHINGTON WEB SITES

189 Washington Statutes are referenced in
Guiding Those Left Behind In Washington

Each state has its own set of laws relating to the settlement of a person's estate. The Washington laws that are referenced in this book are very different from the laws of other states. The author is in now in the process of "translating" *Guiding Those Left Behind* for the rest of the states; that is, to write a book that incorporates the laws of the state into a book that describes how to settle the affairs of a decedent in that state.

Guiding Those Left Behind is currently available for the following states:

ALABAMA, ARIZONA, CALIFORNIA, FLORIDA
GEORGIA, HAWAII, ILLINOIS, INDIANA
MASSACHUSETTS, MARYLAND, MICHIGAN
MINNESOTA, MISSOURI, MISSISSIPPI
NEW JERSEY, NEW YORK, NORTH CAROLINA, OHIO
PENNSYLVANIA, SOUTH CAROLINA, TENNESSEE
TEXAS, VIRGINIA, WASHINGTON, WISCONSIN

To check whether this book is currently available for other states call Eagle Publishing Company of Boca at
(800) 824-0823
- or -
Visit our Web site http://www.eaglepublishing.com

BOOK REVIEWS FROM DIFFERENT STATES

ARIZONA

Ben T. Traywick of the Tombstone Epitaph said "This book is an excellent reference book that simplifies all the necessary tasks that must be done when there is a death in the family. There is even an explanation as to how you can arrange your own estate so that your heirs will not be left with a multitude of nagging problems." "The reviewer has been going through probate for two years with no end yet in sight. This book at the beginning two year ago would have helped immensely."

CALIFORNIA

Margot Petit Nichols of the Carmel Pine Cone called it a ". . .TRULY RIVETING READ." " . . . I could scarcely put it down." "This is a book that we should all have, either on our book shelves or thoughtfully placed with our important papers."

FLORIDA

Maryhelen Clague of the Tampa Tribune Times wrote "Amelia Pohl has created a handy, self-help guide that illustrates the necessary steps that must be taken when someone dies, a guide that is easy to read, extremely clear and simple to refer to when the need arises."

NEW YORK

Saul Friedman of NEWSDAY said "And one section that should be read by readers of any age, suggests and describes how to create an 'If I Die' file to point the way to your vital papers and policies, to minimize the problems and costs for your survivors. Alas, not even you boomers will live forever."

Beyond Grief To Acceptance and Peace

AMELIA E. POHL and the noted psychologist BARBARA J. SIMMONDS, Ph.d, have written a book for those families who have suffered a loss.

Beyond Grief To Acceptance and Peace explains:
- ◇ What to say to the bereaved
- ◇ How to help a child through the loss
- ◇ Strategies to adjust to a new lifestyle
- ◇ When and where to seek assistance.

The second edition of this 80 page book is now available for $10.95 plus shipping and handling. You can order the book using the following discount coupon for a total of $10.

DISCOUNT COUPON

Please send me a copy of Beyond Grief To Acceptance and Peace

☐ I am enclosing a check for $10.
☐ Charge this to my _____ credit card
(Visa, Master, Discover)
Credit Card no. _____
Expiration date: _____

Name _____
Address _____
_____

Mail this coupon to:
EAGLE PUBLISHING COMPANY OF BOCA
4199 N. Dixie Hwy. #2
Boca Raton, FL 33431

A Will is Not Enough Washington

Many people who have a Will think that they have their affairs in order. They believe that their Will can take care of any problem that may arise. But the primary function of a Will is to distribute property to people named in a Will. A Will cannot:

➪   Manage your personal debt

➪   Limit your business debt

➪   Provide care for a minor or disabled child

➪   Appoint someone to make your health care decisions should you be unable to do so

➪   Appoint someone to handle your finances should you be unable to do so

➪   Arrange to pay for your health care should you need long term nursing care

➪   Help you qualify for MEDICAID.

AMELIA E. POHL, Esq. has writen a book that explains how to do all of these things in the state of Washington. The result of her efforts is

A Will is Not Enough in Washington.

This new book is a continuation of this book. It builds on basic Estate Planning concepts introduced in Chapter 7 of this book and then goes on to introduce other, more sophisticated, Estate Planning methods.

Although the topics are sophisticated, the writing style is the same as this book. It is written in plain English. It is intended for use by the average person.

Readers of this book can purchase *A Will is Not Enough in Washington* for $25. The price includes shipping and handling. To order, call Eagle Publishing Company at

(800) 824-0823.

It is the goal of EAGLE PUBLISHING COMPANY to keep our publications fresh.

As we receive information about changes to the federal or Washington law we will post an update to this edition at our Web site:

http://www.eaglepublishing.com